Newcastle United's
~~greatest~~ ever players
^
WORST

ISBN 978-1480157606

www.peternuttall.net

Contents

Special Features

Preface

Since the first professional footballer pulled on the black and white stripes of Newcastle United, fans have been thrilled by the outlandish skill of nippy midfielders, exhilarated by the breath-taking goals of some of the world's greatest strikers and triumphant in the capture of another trophy to add to the other prestigious cups and awards collected during Newcastle United's glittering history. However, fans have also been confounded by the inept passing ability of inexplicably expensive footballers and devastated by their inability to convert clear-cut chances into goals. These unwieldy exponents of incompetence all seem to possess the same eerie gift of being able to supress every rudimentary footballing instinct when participating in a game of moderate importance to the Geordie nation.

This book is a litany of those who failed in black and white stripes whether performing to the extremes of their ability to try and win the hearts and minds of the Geordies or simply 'making an appearance' in an attempt to justify their wages. Through nothing other than notoriety, you'll hear the names of Frank Pingel and Albert Luque mentioned in the drinking establishments of Newcastle almost as many times as those of Les Ferdinand, Alan Shearer and Peter Beardsley.

The criteria for inclusion in this book go much further than the players' statistics. As fans who followed Newcastle in the 1999/2000 season will know, Kevin Gallacher was never in danger of becoming the most fruitful striker in Newcastle United's history but the affable Scot gradually eased his way into many fans' affections by playing an important role in Sir Bobby Robson's ship-steadying first season. Stats will of course play some part in a player being universally derided by the fans, but it is rare for a striker who is truly awful to clock up thirty six appearances without finding the net. Tony Cunningham's paltry four league goals in forty seven games certainly tells its own story but George Reilly's ten strikes from thirty one league games would sound like a reasonable return unless you were one of the unfortunate few who paid money to watch him in 1985 having been brought up watching the likes of Malcolm McDonald, Kevin Keegan and Terry Hibbitt.

All the players in this book have at one time made a Newcastle fan hold their head in their hands; some just by having their name read out over the tannoy during the announcement of the first team. Some players didn't even have to take to the field to cause universal despair among those gathered before kick-off. These are players who were able to cause thirty-odd thousand people to shout the word 'yeah' followed by the word 'ahr' every single time they 'unleashed' a shot at goal. These are players who wouldn't be given a top trump card in the 'People who played for Newcastle United' edition, even if there were 600 cards in the deck. It's not that they were all bad players; in Jon Dahl Tomasson's case, he left Newcastle and went on to become one of Europe's greatest ever forwards, it's just that when they were wearing the black and white stripes, they were simply dreadful. If every time they touched the ball it ended up in the pond in Leazes Park or if every single one of their shortcomings caused your blood to turn into steam, they're here.

As fans, we're all willing to give new signings time to settle or a player from the youth team time to find his feet, but as you'll see, it's sometimes clear from their first kick of the ball that they're destined to perpetually disappoint you.

Andreas Andersson

Toon years : 1998 – 1999
Position : Forward
Games played : 32
Goals : 4
Signed by : Kenny Dalglish
Transfer fee paid : £3 million
Transfer fee received : £2 million

Time in Toon

With a forward line that boasted the likes of Ian Rush, Jon Dahl
Tomasson and Temuri Ketsbaia, (managing 3 goals between them by
Christmas in the 1997/1998 season and with Newcastle sitting 10th in the
league), something drastic was needed in an attempt to return to the
heady days of Kevin Keegan's exciting, ruthless and potent attacking
football. Unfortunately Kenny Dalglish decided (after scouting Europe
for the previous twelve months) to spend three million of the twenty two
million pounds he'd received from the sales of Paul Kitson, Lee Clark,
Robbie Elliott, David Ginola, Les Ferdinand and Tino Asprilla on AC
Milan reserve Andreas Andersson. After one start and thirteen substitute
appearances for the Milan club, he confidently stepped up to the plate for
Newcastle; unfortunately it was a plate of headbands to keep a mop of
floppy blonde 80's hair out of his eyes. His first goal for the club came
on his tenth appearance; Alan Shearer hit the crossbar from a few yards
out in a home game against Barnsley in April 1998. Andreas was on hand
to head the ball into an unguarded net from six yards. His second goal
came just five days later at Old Trafford when a quite obviously offside
Gary Speed headed the ball into Andreas' path. Everyone stopped,
waiting for the flag and whistle except Mr. Andersson (the scene
ironically playing out like one of those slow-motion scenes from *The
Matrix*) who powered the ball into Manchester United's net like his hair
depended on it.

Best Moment

Andreas managed a feat that had eluded many a Newcastle United striker
in the past; finding the net in the Premier League at Stamford Bridge. It
was only Newcastle's 6th Premier League away fixture against the Blues
and they went there with the less-than-inspirational knowledge that not
only was Kenny 'everyone in your own half' Dalglish attempting to
mastermind the operation but they'd only managed to register two goals

in the previous five attempts (and one of those was scored by fullback Marc Hottiger). A familiar wave of bleak despondency washed across the sea of black and white clad fans in the away end when future Magpie Celestine Babayaro put Chelsea in front with his first goal for the club after Stuart Pearce had managed to stop perennial Toon-disappointer Gus Poyet's shot on the line. Up stepped Mr. Andersson to save the day in his own unique haphazard way. He didn't equalise through the use of elaborate cunning, skill and nifty touches which mesmerised the Chelsea defence – it was because of another slip from Newcastle's favourite opposing defender, Michael Duberry that let him in to score. Alan Shearer steered a tame-looking header across the penalty area that caused Duberry to, well... 'do a Duberry' and allowed Andersson to slot a right footed shot into the opposite corner of the goal past Ed De Goey.

Worst Moment

If only Isaac Newton were alive to see it, he would have rethought his theories on classical mechanics. Andreas was bearing down on the Sheffield United goal in the first half of the FA Cup Semi-Final in 1998. With the ball in front of him, sitting up nicely to be lashed into the net from sixteen yards past a petrified looking Alan Kelly, he managed to defy the laws of physics. The nerve which sent the 'boot it' message from his brain to his feet misfired and instead sent the message 'tangle yourselves up then point towards the sky', which they obeyed expertly. During this exhibition of ungainly behaviour, one of his boots managed to connect with the ball and send it on an unlikely path towards the unguarded Sheffield goal. However, defender Lee Sandford managed to get back in time to clear and preserve parity. Alan Shearer did manage to get on the score-sheet later in the game to save Andreas' blushes and send Newcastle to an episode of greater embarrassment at Wembley.

Verdict

A player with obvious ability, scoring at both international and Champions' League level (and scoring almost a goal a game in his time with IFK Gothenburg), he always seemed to look lost and bewildered by proceedings during Premier League games. The arrival of Andersson midway through the 1997/1998 term coincided with Newcastle's second lowest return of top flight goals in a season. The 35 goals they managed were second only to the 32 scored in the relegation season of 1988/1989 when only one player managed to score over 4 league goals; that being the haphazard Mirandinha. Similarly, in 1997/1998 only the 'mature' John Barnes managed to score more than four league goals. So perhaps Andreas was more a victim of Newcastle's lack of creativity and Kenny

Dalglish's negative tactics than his lack of skill with a football. Andy Carroll is all too aware of the effect Mr. Dalglish can have on a promising striker's career.

Dave Beasant

Toon years : 1988
Position : Goalkeeper
Games played : 26
Clean sheets : 6
Signed by : Willie McFaul
Transfer fee paid : £750,000
Transfer fee received : £800,000

Time in Toon

May 1988, John Aldridge steps up to equalise Lawrie Sanchez's first half opener from the penalty spot and put Liverpool back in with a chance of lifting the FA Cup; cue Dave Beasant's telescopic arms. The person responsible for recommending the leggy goalkeeper to Willie McFaul was clearly watching the game on TV that day. Beasant fell to his left and palmed John Aldridge's penalty around the post to help his team to a 1-0 victory. This one save alone seemed to be enough to convince Gordon McKeag to sanction the £750,000 needed to sign him (a record fee for a goalkeeper at that time). Newcastle weren't in any great need for a new goalkeeper in the summer of 1988 since Gary Kelly had kept eight clean sheets and conceded only forty nine goals in thirty seven league games to help Newcastle to an 8th place finish in 1987/1988.

Arriving in a hail of optimism along with Wimbledon team mate Andy Thorn, Beasant started in the Newcastle goal for their first game of the season away to Everton. His first task (with the season just 32 seconds old) was to palm Graeme Sharp's punt at goal into the path of Toffees debutant Tony Cottee who rolled the ball into the empty net from ten yards. Beasant's second task was to pick the ball out of the net and return it to the centre circle, as were his third, fourth and fifth tasks. For the entire ninety minutes, his face mimicked those of the travelling contingent, painted with a look of sheer bewilderment. Welcome to Newcastle United.

Best Moment

Choosing Beasant's best moment is tricky. It was either the day he left Newcastle for Chelsea or the save he made in the 2-1 victory away to Liverpool. With the score tied at 1-1 in that game, Peter Beardsley shimmied the ball onto his right foot and drifted a beautiful cross into the box. Gary Ablett managed a skimmed header onto John Aldridge who was unmarked in front of goal. With the nearest defender six yards away,

Aldridge jerked his head forward and directed the ball towards the top left hand corner of the goal. Managing to leave the ground for the first and only time in his Newcastle career, Beasant reached up a hand and acrobatically tipped the ball onto the angle of post and crossbar.

Worst Moment

Whilst keeping the Newcastle goal, Beasant had a habit of diving before the ball had been kicked in his direction. In the 2-2 draw away to Charlton, Paul Williams found himself clean through in the second half. Instead of standing tall and relying on his reflexes, Beasant decided to have a lie down a full three seconds before Williams took his shot. A goal was only prevented on this occasion by a late Andy Thorn lunge.

Among the plethora of sub-standard goalkeeping however is the moment when most Magpies fans made their minds up about the bubble-permed custodian of Newcastle's goal. For all his six foot four inches, Beasant seemed unable to let his boots leave the ground when reaching for high balls. He infrequently took crosses and found that attacking players were attempting to chip him with increasing frequency as the season wore on. In the 2-0 home defeat to Norwich, Robert Fleck found himself free in the penalty area with only Beasant to beat. He chipped the ball, which rose no higher than the crossbar, causing it to sail over the despairing left hand of the goalkeeper and across the goal line despite the best efforts of Andy Thorn to clear it with a spectacular scissor kick.

Verdict

Dave Beasant could and should have been Newcastle's Peter Schmeichel. Picking up England caps and succeeding Matthew Le Tissier as the Southampton fans' player of the season in 1996, when on form, Beasant could make breath-taking saves. This ability was tempered however by his penchant for mistakes such as the two moments of madness when playing for Chelsea against Norwich in 1992. His favourite tactic was to leave his eighteen yard box with the ball at his feet and launch it up-field into the opposition's box. This worked wonders when playing for Wimbledon with the likes of John Fashanu challenging panicked defenders in the air. With the five foot seven Mirandinha, five foot seven John Hendrie and the five foot seven John Robertson, this party piece could never have borne fruit at Newcastle. Judging him purely as a guardian of the Newcastle goal however, conceding 35 goals in 20 league games (conceding two or more goals in over half of the games he played in) combined with the fact Newcastle only scored 32 league goals that season (the poorest return in their top flight history) meant Dave Beasant's departure to second division Chelsea only seven months after joining Newcastle, was inevitable. To be fair on Beasant, there were times when the central defensive partnership of Andy Thorn and Kevin Scott went missing. Sometimes it was difficult to spot either of them on the field while the exposed Beasant was left trying to save from an attacker with a clear sight of goal and at least two other unmarked forwards in attendance.

It may not surprise you to know that Beasant dropped a bottle of salad cream on his foot and missed two months of the 1993/1994 season; when it fell out of the cupboard, it sent him the wrong way.

Jean-Alain Boumsong

Toon years : 2005 - 2006
Position : Central defender
Games played : 59
Goals : 0
Signed by : Graeme Souness
Transfer fee paid : £8 million
Transfer fee received : £3.5 million

Time in Toon

Newcastle purchased Jean-Alain for the hefty sum of £8 million pounds from Rangers after the Scottish club had signed him only half a year earlier on a free transfer. Boumsong's time in a black and white shirt started rather promisingly on paper, helping the team to four clean sheets in his first seven games, six of which were victories including 1-0 successes against Chelsea in the FA Cup and Liverpool in the league. Things were not as they seemed however. His debut away to Yeading in the FA Cup was less than assured, looking positively terrified at one point in the first half when receiving a pass from Titus Bramble on the edge of his own eighteen yard box. It didn't take long for Titus' erratic defensive style to influence Boumsong's own performances. Playing in the same team as Amdy Faye and Albert Luque was never going instil him with the greatest confidence but it was in his seventh game that Newcastle fans started noticing Boumsong's partiality for making mistakes. A 1-1 draw away to Portsmouth was followed by five straight defeats which included the Bowyer vs. Dyer boxing match and an abject 4-1 defeat in the FA Cup Semi-Final against Manchester United.

Best Moment

Captaining Newcastle in a 3-1 victory over Fulham in May 2005, Boumsong said at the time that wearing the armband was one of the proudest moments of his career.

Worst Moment

Mid-march 2006; Newcastle were 2-1 down to Liverpool. The ball fell out of the sky a few metres from Newcastle's eighteen yard box and bounced innocuously near Boumsong's right foot. Not since the Battle of Hastings has anyone so fatally misjudged the flight of something.

Running back towards his own goal, Boumsong contorted his body and swung a leg with the power of one hundred Buffalo. His foot missed the ball completely but the power of the swing created a slip-stream which aided Peter Crouch's burst into the area. Boumsong managed to perform a 180 degree turn in order to wrap both arms around Crouch outside the area in order to somehow atone for his mistake. Cleverly though, Crouch made it into the area before collapsing in a melee of arms and legs reminiscent of the opening stages of a game of *pick-up sticks*. Despite the presence of Robbie Elliot not five yards to the right of the incident, Boumsong was adjudged by referee Mike Riley to have committed a professional foul and showed the Newcastle player a red card (Newcastle's sixth red card of the season). Boumsong slapped both hands to his face, realising that this was the very last mistake he would ever make in a Newcastle shirt. Mike Riley turned and waved an indignant arm at Boumsong, instructing him to stop reflecting on his own ineptitude and leave the field. Unable to neither accept nor believe what had happened, Boumsong hung around behind the goal as the penalty was spotted up, hoping the referee would rescind the red card and tell him he was only joking. Even Shay Given glanced back at the forlorn and broken figure behind his goal without sympathy. Boumsong appeared in Newcastle's next league game, a 3-1 defeat to Charlton (though he was not directly responsible for any of the goals conceded) but was absent from all subsequent starting elevens as Newcastle won six of their last seven games to qualify for the Intertoto Cup. That run included the 4-1 success at the Stadium of Light which even the event of Boumsong coming on as an 88th minute substitute couldn't spoil.

Verdict

Boumsong's name is frequently mentioned by Newcastle fans whenever the topics of 'biggest wastes of money' or 'worst ever players' are discussed. While looking assured and comfortable on the ball at times in his first season, he made so many mistakes in his second season it seemed he'd completely forgotten he was a footballer. He was often found miskicking the ball at crucial moments, sliding in for challenges (missing both ball and player), hoofing the ball directly up into the air when he finally did make contact or fatally and frequently missing the ball completely like his feet were made of ether. Boumsong even got in the way of a goal-bound Alan Shearer effort away to Liverpool in what seemed like confirmation that he didn't want Newcastle to win another game ever again. Whilst he was erratic at times, his mistakes didn't lead to as many opposition goals as you may think. Certainly, Newcastle fans have had to watch far worse than the six foot three French international but none were so expensive. When judging a central defender, it's important to look at his partner. For those fans who thought Nikos Dabizas could be poor at times, remember that he had Titus Bramble alongside him and often found himself two against one when Warren Barton had decided to leave the comfort of his own half and decide to saunter back once he'd inevitably lost possession. Boumsong also played alongside the young and often error prone Steven Taylor, which tore Shay Given's nerves and patience to shreds. That said, the collective sigh of relief that emanated from Newcastle was audible in Turin when Boumsong's transfer to Juventus was confirmed. Whether he was suffering from a lack of confidence or motivation, whether plagued by personal problems or simply because of the way he was managed by the coaching staff, Boumsong will always be regarded by watchers of the Premier League as one of the worst defenders ever to participate.

Titus Bramble

Toon years : 2002 - 2007
Position : Central Defender
Games played : 158
Goals : 7
Signed by : Sir Bobby Robson
Transfer fee paid : £5 million
Transfer fee received : Released

Time in Toon

Titus was a popular Newcastle player, in that he allowed many supporters to finally complete their copies of the 'I-spy book of footballing mistakes'. Blessed with the physical presence of a brick-outhouse and sometimes playing with the ability of Franz Beckenbauer, Bramble was prone to the kind of mistake someone who'd never previously encountered a football would make. Just as Kryptonite causes Superman to lose his powers, it seemed a similar thing happened to Bramble when the ball was in contact with grass. In the air, he was almost unbeatable, but whenever a through-ball was played along the ground within a few yards of him, his feet may as well have been on back-to-front. He was part of the Newcastle team who succumbed to a 5-2 defeat by Blackburn in 2002, a 6-2 reverse against Manchester United in 2003 which effectively ended any title aspirations Newcastle had that season, a 5-0 defeat at Chelsea later that year followed by a 4-0 reverse at the same venue almost a year later, the 4-1 loss in Lisbon with Newcastle 2-0 up on aggregate, another defeat at Stamford bridge, 3-0 this time in 2005, the 3-0 loss at Manchester City that cost Graeme Souness his job and the 2-0 loss against AZ Alkmaar in 2007 which was his third to last game for the club and saw us eliminated despite leading 4-2 going into the second leg. Admittedly, those stats are loaded because he played in many more victories than he did defeats, but when the games that really mattered came around, the Newcastle defence, which included Bramble, was left wanting.

Best Moment

Scoring his sixth Newcastle goal on the final day of the 2005/2006 season at the Gallowgate end, Titus's goal was enough to defeat then Premier League Champions Chelsea 1-0 which meant Newcastle qualified for the Intertoto Cup and a chance of UEFA Cup football the following season. Emre swung a corner into the box which met the head of Amdy Faye.

14

Whether intentional or not, his header found the feet of Bramble who lashed the ball into the net from a few yards out.

Worst Moment

One of Newcastle's better performances at Highbury in September 2003 ended in a 3-2 defeat partly due to a truly amateur performance by Bramble. In the 17th minute of the game, Arsenal full-back Lauren received the ball on the right, level with the Newcastle eighteen yard box and with Laurent Robert ten yards away from him (and Olivier Bernard even further away) delivered a poor cross into the box. Bramble watched the ball as it floated towards him and landed inches away from his left foot. With an expression of hysterical glee, Titus swung his leg at the ball, missing completely and allowed it to bounce across the six yard box to the unmarked Thierry Henry who gratefully tapped the ball into the empty net at the far post.

Verdict

Titus' middle name is Malachi – which in Hebrew means 'messenger'. He certainly sent messages to the Newcastle fans whenever he played and it was rarely good news. Fans can only dream what might have been possible had Sylvain Distin signed for Newcastle after his loan spell instead of choosing Kevin Keegan and Manchester City who could guarantee a first team slot at centre back. Instead, Sir Bobby Robson signed Titus Bramble, and the rest as they say…

Claudio Cacapa

Toon years : 2007 - 2009
Position : Central Defender
Games played : 29
Goals : 2
Signed by : Sam Allardyce
Transfer fee paid : Free
Transfer fee received : Free

Time in Toon

Along with the promise of much needed stability and discipline brought
to the club by Sam Allardyce in 2007, came players such as Mark 'when I
feel like it' Viduka, David 'out of my depth' Rozehnal, Alan 'sliding
tackle' Smith, Geremi 'limps *onto* the pitch' Njitap and Claudio Cacapa.
Cacapa came to Newcastle with a good reputation. Being Brazilian
helped excite the fans, as did winning a Golden Ball award for being the
best defender in the Brazilian league in 1999. He then captained Lyon to
five French *ligue 1* titles playing 125 games and scoring 7 times. What
could possibly go wrong?

He signed for Newcastle on a free transfer and made his full
debut against Barnsley in the League Cup. In this game he looked quick,
intelligent, positionally sound, good in the tackle and assured when
receiving and passing the ball. However, he was a defender and being a
defender playing for Newcastle United means career-threatening disaster
is never far away. A bafflingly poor eighteen minutes against Portsmouth
in November 2007 was followed by persistent injury problems and
inconsistency of form. Injury made a run in the first team impossible the
following season and when his contract ran out in 2009, he was released.

Best Moment

On the 16th January 2008, Newcastle played Stoke City in an FA Cup
third round replay at St. James' Park. After Michael Owen had given
Newcastle the lead and a red card for Emre threatened to spoil the party
atmosphere, Charles N'Zogbia floated a cross into the box from a corner
which met the forehead of the onrushing Cacapa. With the force of a run-
away train, the ball hit the back of the Stoke net. The delight on Cacapa's
face has never been surpassed in living history; not even by the faces of
Newcastle fans when news broke that Kevin Keegan was returning as
Newcastle United manager earlier that day. Cacapa turned and ran back
towards his own goal punching the air and screaming glee up into the

sky. Not quite as mad as Temuri Ketsbaia's protest against commercialism, but the possibility of turning just four wins in the previous 17 Allardyce-supervised games (not including the post-Sam 6-0 defeat at old Trafford just four days earlier) into 'one in one' for Kevin Keegan, opened a Pandora's box of excitement somewhere inside Cacapa's soul for all to witness.

Worst Moment

Even the kindest and most tolerant fan would admit that Claudio managed to usurp Titus Bramble for the 'defensive lapse of the decade' award twice in the same game when he lined up against Portsmouth at St. James' Park in November 2007. After just nine minutes, a hopeful punt up field by Portsmouth seemed to be dropping out of the sky directly onto Cacapa's head. His concentration was broken temporarily and he allowed the ball to bounce. Completely lost, he allowed Benjani to nip in and fire a shot past Steve Harper to make it 2-0. Two minutes later, a misjudged header by Steven Taylor put Cacapa in trouble and before he could react, Utaka had brushed him aside and taken the ball around the bewildered Steve Harper to make it 3-0.

Verdict

Cacapa only appeared in nineteen first team games in his first season and six in his second. It was evident that he possessed the strength and composure needed to be a very good centre half; unfortunately, glimpses of this ability were infrequent. It may seem a little unfair to include Cacapa in this book but when something like the Portsmouth incident happens to a player who is then plagued by injuries and never plays well enough to allow the fans to forgive and forget, he will inevitably find himself in the 'nearly' bin alongside Marcelino and Albert Luque.

So close?

Why?

A topic of conversation which crops up frequently between Newcastle United fans starved of major trophy success since 1969 centres around *that* season. The season when the black and white planets aligned and Newcastle United stormed into a twelve point lead at the top of the Premier League. But what went wrong? Well, Manchester United managed to pick up sixteen more points than Newcastle did after that twelve point lead was established for a start. Football however is a game of opinions and many claim the signing of Faustino Asprilla caused Newcastle to wobble, upsetting the balance of the team or even upsetting the players themselves. Some say the sending off of David Ginola against Arsenal in the League Cup in January 1996 affected the Frenchman for the rest of the season and his form dipped as a result. However, all these things are subjective depending on your own prejudices and viewpoints. What I will do in this section is present the facts of the 1995/1996 season and allow you to draw your own conclusions.

1. Newcastle lost two of the first nineteen league games of the season. One at their bogey ground of The Dell and the other at Stamford Bridge; both by one goal to nil.
2. Newcastle conceded sixteen goals in those first nineteen games, scoring forty in reply.
3. The twentieth game of the season was away to Manchester United. Newcastle lost that game 2-0, losing Keith Gillespie midway through the first half to injury.
4. After scoring 12 goals in 8 consecutive games, Les Ferdinand had the chance to break Newcastle's all-time goal-scoring record away at Tottenham Hotspur in October 1995. With the scores at 1-1 in the 93rd minute, Peter Beardsley beat Dean Austin and threaded a ball through for Ferdinand who found himself with the ball at his feet and nobody near him sixteen yards from goal with only Ian Walker to beat. He shaped to shoot with his right foot but seemed to change his mind, readjusted his left foot and then by the time he made contact with the ball it had rolled between Walker's legs, bounced up and when Ferdinand finally knocked the ball goalwards, a Tottenham defender was on hand to block it. The game ended 1-1.

5. Manchester United won fifteen and drew the other four of their home games that season. Newcastle won seventeen, drew one and lost one. The defeat? 1-0 to Manchester United.

6. Newcastle lost eight games while Manchester United lost six.

7. Newcastle had the worst defensive record in the top five, conceding 37 goals. Arsenal's was best with 32, Liverpool with 34, Aston Villa and Manchester United both conceded 35.

8. Shaka Hislop conceded 15 goals in 17 games before he was injured, a ratio of 0.88 per game. Pavel Srnicek then took over when Shaka was injured in the 1-0 defeat at Chelsea in December 1995. Pavel conceded 17 in 14 games (1.2 per game) before Hislop returned. Hislop then played in the final seven games of the season conceding five goals meaning his final ratio for the season was 20 goals in 24 games (0.83). Had Srnicek matched Hislop's ratio it would have meant Newcastle conceding four less goals during his time between the posts and could have resulted in clawing back the five points needed to finish top of the table.

9. Since signing in February 1996, Faustino Asprilla appeared in each of Newcastle's remaining fourteen league games that season. Newcastle won just three of the first nine games that Asprilla played in, losing five. They'd only lost three of the previous twenty four without Asprilla. They finished the season winning only 6 of those last 14.

10. Les Ferdinand scored 20 goals in his first 23 Premier League games for Newcastle before Asprilla's arrival at the club. Excluding the away game at Middlesbrough where Asprilla was used as a substitute, Ferdinand scored 4 goals in the next 13 games alongside Asprilla, with Tino himself only contributing 3 goals. Without Asprilla, Ferdinand's goal ratio in the Premier League was 0.87 – with Asprilla starting alongside him it fell drastically to 0.31; add in Asprilla's goals and this only raises the ratio for Newcastle's front two to 0.5, still well short of what Ferdinand was achieving with Peter Beardsley alongside him providing the service.

11. The only defeat in the last seven games came at Blackburn via two goals from the right boot of Graeme Fenton. Even if Newcastle had picked up those three points, they would still have finished one point behind Champions Manchester United.

12. If Newcastle had picked up maximum points from the last two games instead of playing out two 1-1 draws against Nottingham Forest and Tottenham Hotspur, Manchester United would still have finished top on goal-difference.

13. Keegan admitted after the season finished that David Batty was the main reason Newcastle stayed so close to Manchester United, discounting the opinion that Newcastle had lost the league, more that they couldn't stop Manchester United from winning it.

Despite what was a desperately disappointing last three months of the season following an absolutely stunning start, fans were able to reflect on some sublime football and some of the best entertainment they'd seen in the last forty years. Keegan even said the highlight of his season was the 4-3 defeat to Liverpool in April 1996; just to be involved in a game like that was testament to the way he wanted his teams to play football.

Tony Cunningham

Toon years : 1985 - 1987
Position : Centre Forward
Games played : 51
Goals : 6
Signed by : Jack Charlton
Transfer fee paid : Free Transfer
Transfer fee received : £25,000

Time in Toon

Tony Cunningham was signed by Jack Charlton who had an odd recruitment policy whilst manager of Newcastle United. With players such as Peter Beardsley and Chris Waddle at his disposal he decided to sign Tony Cunningham and George 'Mavis' Reilly to play a 'large and large' partnership up front when it seemed Newcastle could finally build a title-challenging team around two of England's best players and a young Paul Gascoigne who only a few years later would be regarded by many as one of the best players in the world.

Tony scored one top flight goal in his first season from thirteen starts. He scored one goal in ten league starts (and seven substitute appearances) the following season. Any fan would be ecstatic if they were told their first-choice centre forward would score twice as many goals next season as they had this; well, in Tony's case, he did! He scored two goals in fourteen league starts in the 1986-87 season, 'helping' Newcastle to a 17th place finish in Division 1, just five points clear of relegation. His first goal for the club came in his fourth game for Newcastle, home to Watford in March 1985. He then had to wait twenty one league games to register his second.

Best Moment

Joining Newcastle was the pinnacle of his career. Enough said.

Worst Moment

Considering his plethora of non-descript and anonymous appearances in a black and white shirt, to decide on his worst moment is difficult. Instead, I've chosen the worst moment for Newcastle fans watching a side containing the talents of Mr. Cunningham. April 21st 1986, Upton Park; a tale of three 'keepers. Early in the first half, West Ham won a free kick near Newcastle's right-hand corner flag and Alan 'Aslan' Devonshire steadied himself before floating the ball into the box. With Tony standing stock-still in the centre of the Newcastle penalty, he watched the ball glide over his head and drop onto the boot of Alvin Martin who tapped it into the net from less than a yard out.

A few minutes later Martin Thomas managed to push a tame right wing cross into his own net for the second goal and was then beaten by an innocuous forty yard toe-ender which inexplicably went through the goal posts dead-centre at chest height. The fourth West Ham goal came when Glenn Roeder performed a manoeuvre which Kieron Dyer would later emulate in Barcelona's *Camp Nou* sixteen years later. The ball appeared over Roeder's left shoulder and for reasons best known to himself, flicked his left leg out and sent the ball past Martin Thomas.

In the second half, Thomas attempted to take an easy cross on his six yard box but fumbled the ball spectacularly and then had to scamper after it like an escaped chicken. He caught up to the ball on the right hand side of the box where Tony Cottee attempted to dispossess Thomas by sitting on his shoulder. After several minutes of treatment Thomas had to leave the field.

He was replaced in goal by winger Ian Stewart, which seemed at the time like a blessing, given that Thomas was having one of the worst games of his career. Stewart made one save, almost dislocating a hand in the process and then (after watching Martin Thomas' performance and copying it to the letter) punched the next shot into his own goal to make it 5-0. Stewart then went off, nursing his dislodged metacarpals, to be replaced by Peter 'runs like a cheetah' Beardsley. Beardsley immediately made a save and then looked on as Billy Whitehurst drilled the ball towards the West Ham goal at the other end. It looked to everyone in the ground that it had been cleared off the line but the referee took pity and the goal was given to make it 5-1. Typically, the away fans jumped about with hallucinogenic delight believing a repeat of the 5-5 draw with Queens Park Rangers only two years previous was on the cards.

However, West Ham's sixth goal was nodded in at the far post by future Newcastle striker Paul Goddard; McAvennie added the seventh with a simple header from four yards out and the eighth from a penalty. Oddly, when the penalty was conceded with the score at 7-1, Tony Cunningham led a five-man charge towards the referee in remonstration, arguing for a good minute about the decision. By this stage, even the staunchest Newcastle fans had given up on this game as a defeat, but not Tony Cunningham. His desperate pleadings seemed to go a lot deeper than a superficial sense of injustice at the fact it was never a penalty. His pleading seemed to be laced with the same sense of devastation that the score might turn from a 7-1 drubbing into an 8-1 annihilation as you'd feel if Sunderland had just beaten you 2-0 in the play-off Semi-Final and then got promoted to the top division after a defeat at Wembley on a technicality. If only he'd injected the same zeal and passion up the other end of the field when the ball was there to be won, the score line might have been different. It was a night when every player's first touch was a pass to a West Ham player and Tony Cunningham had exactly eight touches of the ball – each of those coming when he kicked off following a West Ham goal.

Verdict

Fans who remember watching Tony play will only ever conjure a mental picture of him with a permanent apologetic expression. Whether he'd rolled a side-footer ten yards wide of the post or won a header only to direct it towards his own goal, Tony always looked despondent, as if he was telling himself that he'd do better next time. Unfortunately for him, he only ever did *worse* next time. Almost inevitably, when Cunningham left Tyneside for Blackpool, he scored against Newcastle in the League Cup second round first leg to give Blackpool a 1-0 victory. Cunningham had the strike-rate of a centre back, which as a forward, was never going to earn a photograph on the wall in the 1892 bar at St. James' Park. Whatever his failings, he is still held in higher esteem than certain other, more expensive and more prolific Newcastle strikers.

Wayne Fereday

Toon years : 1989 - 1990
Position : Winger/Full-back
Games played : 41
Goals : 0
Signed by : Jim Smith
Transfer fee paid : £400,000
Transfer fee received : Free Transfer

Time in Toon

After tumbling meekly out of the top division in 1989, Jim Smith had the task of preparing the club for life in Division Two on a tight budget. The Newcastle manager proved he had an eye for a player by bringing the vastly experienced and talented (but at the time, largely unknown to the Newcastle faithful) Mick Quinn to the club alongside former Magpie Mark McGhee to form the best and most consistent strike partnership the fans had seen for a long time. What these two players needed was service from wide areas and so he bought two wingers. John Gallacher arrived at the club and quickly showed the fans what they'd been missing the previous season. He had bags of ability and weighed in with goals and assists alike. Jim also bought Wayne Fereday.

Wayne had played under Jim Smith when they were both at QPR. He'd already brought Kevin Brock with him when he became Newcastle manager, a move which proved good business. There's an old adage which warns 'you should never go back'. Jim did go back however, and bought Fereday to provide service from wide areas. Unfortunately, the term 'never got going' was given a whole new depth of meaning. His debut was discreet; in the 5-2 home victory over Leeds United he was overshadowed by his fellow provider on the other wing, who scored and had an eventful game. Although he racked up over forty appearances for Newcastle even Goalkeeper Tommy Wright had more assists to his name (and more tackles). Unable to go past a man, unable to even attempt to go past a man, it was hard to believe that Fereday's name had once been mentioned in the same breath as that of the full England Squad.

Best Moment

It was Roy Aitken's debut; a home game against Leicester City in 1990. Roy broke up play in the centre of the field, beat two players and then crossed the half way line. He took two more touches before finding

Fereday out on the right wing with a neat pass using the outside of his right foot. With moustache and mullet bristling in the breeze, the unchallenged Fereday floated a ball to the back post where Mark McGhee headed past Hodge in the Leicester goal to make it 1-0. If the moment sounds unspectacular, then that's because it was. However, for those fans watching at the time, the game was one of the most exciting in living memory, eventually turning a 4-2 deficit into a 5-4 win with Mark McGhee's turn and snap shot winning it at the end.

Worst Moment

In his tenth start for Newcastle, Wayne was finally presented with an opportunity to notch his first strike for the club. In the away game at Ipswich Town, he scuttled towards goal with the ball to find that he only had the goalkeeper to beat. He knew that if he scored, it would give him the lift he needed to become a success in a black and white shirt. Everything was in his favour; his calculations were perfect. He considered the wind-speed and direction, his hairstyle's drag factor, the state of the pitch, distance from goal, length of studs, neatness of moustache and the angle of trajectory. He pulled his foot back and side-footed the ball beyond the goalkeeper and the post. He struck a desperate forlorn figure on the Portman Road pitch. The fans present behind the goal that day still speak of seeing that miss douse the dying embers of hope in Fereday's eyes much like the climactic scene from the film *The Terminator* when the robot gets squashed.

Verdict

By his own admission, Fereday's time in a black and white shirt was poor. As fans, we don't know the truth of what goes on behind the scenes but whatever the reason for Fereday's haunted look whenever he had the ball at his feet, it must have been deep rooted as he never again replicated his form for Queens Park Rangers at any of his subsequent clubs. Thankfully, it was fifteen years before the fans saw another player as ineffective in that position; that was when Sam Allardyce had a dream one night that Alan Smith was a right winger. Somehow, Jim Smith managed to use Fereday as a make-weight in the deal that brought Gavin Peacock to Newcastle; now that's magic!

After the sale of Chris Waddle, Newcastle struggled to find a truly effective and consistent wide-man until Kevin Keegan brought Scott Sellars and eventually, David Ginola to the club. For those familiar with the Chinese yin-yang philosophy; David Ginola was 'yin' and Wayne Fereday was 'yang'.

Rob McDonald

Toon years : 1988 – 1989
Position : Midfield
Games played : 15
Goals : 2
Signed by : Colin Suggett

Time in Toon

It was October 1988 and Newcastle were about to embark on a run of six top flight games without scoring a single goal. Colin Suggett had taken over as caretaker manager following the departure of Willie McFaul, a victim of only one extremely fortunate win in the first eight games of the season. Enter Rob McDonald whose debut 'stimulated' Newcastle to achieve a 0-4 Teddy Sheringham inspired defeat away to Millwall followed by goalless draws with Manchester United and Luton Town. The next game brought a rare victory; a 2-1 success over Wimbledon on 10th December courtesy of two John Hendrie goals. These were United's first goals since the three they'd scored against Middlesbrough back in October. However, this victory neatly coincided with the absence of Rob McDonald from the first team, dropping to the bench to accommodate the return of Darren Jackson. He did manage to get on the field in the second half of this game but was powerless to stop Newcastle claiming all three points.

For those who witnessed Rob's muted scurrying in the middle of the St. James' Park pitch (imagine a small child chasing a balloon in the wind) it's almost impossible to believe he'd played for PSV Eindhoven in their league championship winning 1985/1986 season, playing twenty four games and scoring thirteen goals. In his time with PSV, he played alongside Ruud Gullit and no doubt picked up some of the midfield virtuoso's footballing philosophies; those being to perform abjectly whilst employed by Newcastle United and act as a kind of Trojan horse to destroy any remaining optimism left over from the relative success of recent seasons. In 1988 however, Rob didn't have to go out of his way to try and destroy the dreams of the Newcastle fans. He was playing in a team which at times also accommodated Dave Beasant and Frank Pingel, and they were doing quite a good job of destroying the last remaining traces of Geordie optimism themselves.

Best Moment

Rob had a purple patch lasting 20 minutes against Sheffield Wednesday on Boxing Day in 1988. Peeling away at the back post, the unmarked green and yellow clad McDonald managed to nod a Kevin Brock free kick into Kevin Pressman's unguarded net to cancel out David Hirst's opener. Minutes later, he expertly headed a cross into the path of Michael O'Neill who was unmarked in the box. Ian Cranson then lumbered into the back of O'Neill, shoving him into the ball and causing it to ricochet off at least three different parts of his left leg before trundling into the net. O'Neill then had the audacity to raise an arm in celebration and run off to drink in the adulation of the travelling Newcastle fans rather than shrug his shoulders in an embarrassed manner, which would have been a more suitable response.

Worst Moment

McDonald took to the field as a substitute against Southampton in March 1989, replacing the tired-looking and ineffectual Frank Pingel. After watching McDonald for three minutes, it was the only time Newcastle fans had wished Frank Pingel was still on the pitch.

Verdict

Many fine players with a 'Mc' or a 'Mac' at the start of their surname have represented Newcastle United over the years. Malcolm Macdonald, David McCreery, Terry McDermott, Willie McFaul and Mark McGhee to name but a few; Rob however did not follow the tradition. As well as his league goal against Sheffield Wednesday, he found the net for Newcastle in the *Simod Cup*[1] against Watford but Newcastle went on to lose the game 2-1. Given that Rob played in a Newcastle team devoid of confidence or any kind of tangible leadership, he along with those that contrived to win only 3 home games all season and finish rock bottom of Division One, never stood a chance of being a success in his time at Newcastle.

[1]*The sponsored name of the Full Members Cup, a competition which was created when English teams were banned from competing in European competition following the Heysel stadium disaster.*

Christian Bassedas

Toon years : 2000 - 2003
Position : Midfielder
Games played : 33
Goals : 1
Signed by : Sir Bobby Robson
Transfer fee paid : £4.1 million
Transfer fee received : Free

Time in Toon

When Sir Bobby Robson became Newcastle manager at the end of 1999 he introduced a policy of looking to the Americas (primarily the southern parts) for players. He was blinded by the glittering tradition both Brazil and Argentina had for producing players capable of winning a World Cup every other year. There was also the fact that Mexico, Paraguay, Columbia and Chile also featured in the top twenty of FIFA's world rankings in 2000.

In came Brazilian Fumaca on loan, Paraguayan Diego 'Sparrowhawk' Gavilán for £2m and Brazilian attacking midfielder Paolo Baier for a trial. The hope was that these players would reach the heights of their black and white clad South American predecessors George Robledo, Faustino Asprilla, Nolberto Solano or even Mirandinha. However, they all fell wretchedly short of even the latter's less-than-overwhelming contribution. Nevertheless, Sir Bobby's unsuccessful forays into the South American market didn't deter the Newcastle boss and in the summer of 2000, in came Daniel Cordone for half a million pounds along with fellow Argentinian Christian Bassedas who was signed from *Velez Sarsfield* in Buenos Aires for just over four million pounds. Bassedas had won various trophies with his former club and even represented Argentina in their World Cup qualifying campaign.

Another five South American trialists came in that summer, of which only Pablo Bonvín was invited back on loan. Despite these unexceptional signings, one sojourn to South America did bring back a rough diamond in the shape of Clarence Acuña who despite looking a bit like Feargal Sharkey and wearing an Alice-band in public, always did a steady job.

Bassedas first appeared for Newcastle as a second half substitute, replacing Daniel Cordone during the 4-3 home victory over Bradford City in the League Cup. His first start was in the 1-1 draw with Leicester City, a game in which he conceded the free kick from which Ipswich scored; fouling of all people, Robbie Savage. His Newcastle career consisted of making sure he covered every blade of grass in the centre circle, receiving and giving passes of no more than sixteen inches and generally getting in the way of both the opposition's and his own team-mates' endeavours. Squint and you'd think Scott Parker had signed five years early but had not yet developed any dynamism.

In his first game for Newcastle, Bassedas did look capable of handling himself in the Premier league; that was until he went on to be substituted in all but ten of his next twenty five Premier League starts. His sole positive contribution to the side seemed to be winning free-kicks for being outmuscled – fairly. He didn't win free-kicks in the way Alan Shearer did with wiliness and a wry smile, he won them because he wasn't strong enough to keep possession and fell over at the merest suggestion of a tackle. It remains a mystery to this day what his function in the team was apart from letting Gary Speed make his trademark sojourns up-field in the knowledge that Bassedas dare not cross the halfway line lest he be required to join in the match or break into a sprint.

Best Moment

Bassedas' best moment came in a 3-1 defeat at Stamford Bridge in January 2001. Keiron Dyer baffled Frank Leboeuf in the Chelsea penalty area, got to the byline and crossed the ball into the centre. Shola Ameobi jumped but couldn't connect with the ball and when it finally fell at the feet of Bassedas, he jabbed his foot at the ball and directed it into the far corner to give Newcastle a 1-0 lead.

Worst Moment

Newcastle had drawn 1-1 at home in the FA Cup third round against Aston Villa in January 2001. Off they went to Villa Park for the replay with a fit Marcelino. Newcastle lost 1-0 and Bassedas spent the entire game being knocked off the ball merely by opposition players looking at him sideways, offering nothing to Newcastle's offensive plays and at one point, found himself so far out of position, he seemed to get an attack of agoraphobia and handled the ball for absolutely no reason whatsoever. It got him booked and was equally if not more ludicrous than Steve Watson punching the ball in 1995 against Leeds United and giving away a penalty.

Verdict

In the 2-1 victory over West Ham in April 2001 and the subsequent 1-1 draw away to Sunderland, Bassedas started to look like a player. Not a very good one, but a player nonetheless. This sudden display of mild effectiveness coincided with a mini end-of-season renaissance. After tumbling meekly out of the FA Cup to Aston Villa, Newcastle went on a run of one victory in eight games, scoring just five goals (one of them from the boot of Bassedas). Bassedas then started the next four games from which Newcastle took eight points. In his next game, a 3-0 defeat at Anfield, Bassedas reverted to type.

Intertoto Cup aside, Bassedas started just two more games for Newcastle; the 1-1 season opener against Chelsea in 2001 and a 4-1 home victory against Brentford in the League Cup. His final appearance came off the bench when Tottenham Hotspur undid Sir Bobby's '3-at-the-back' plan with Aaron Hughes shackling the perennial thorn in Newcastle's side, Gus Poyet; inevitably it didn't work and Poyet scored. That was October 2001 and Bassedas made the bench just twice more in the following five games before disappearing from the first team squad altogether. He left in March 2003 when his contract was cancelled but nobody noticed.

Des Hamilton

Toon years : 1997 - 2000
Position : Midfield
Games played : 18
Goals : 1
Signed by : Kenny Dalglish
Transfer fee paid : £1.5 million
Transfer fee received : Free

Time in Toon

Kenny Dalglish's one-man demolition of Newcastle United's first team transcends a generation. Not only did he capture Newcastle's brightest young prospect for many years, Andy Carroll, who moved to Dalglish's Liverpool in 2011 for £35 million, he also signed the disillusioned Peter Beardsley in 1987 during his first term as Liverpool manager. He continued the annihilation in 1997 when he took over from Kevin Keegan as manager. He inexplicably sold all of the players who had made Newcastle a top two team including Lee Clark, Robbie Elliott, David Ginola, Les Ferdinand, Tino Asprilla, John Beresford, Darren Peacock and Shaka Hislop. Using his acute footballing nous, he replaced them with Jon Dahl Tomasson, Alessandro Pistone, Brian Pinas, Ian Rush, Paul Dalglish, Andreas Andersson, Paul Robinson, Lionel Perez, Stephane Guivarc'h, Carl Serrant, Garry Brady and Des Hamilton.

Hamilton's time at Newcastle can be summed up by the results of the games he played in. Of the seven Premiership games he started, Newcastle won one, drew two and lost four. Of the five Premiership games he featured in when coming off the bench, Newcastle won one, drew one and lost three. Newcastle also lost the two Champions League games he started in.

Best Moment

In a League Cup 3rd round game at home to Hull City in 1997, Jon Dahl Tomasson cut across the Hull penalty area and played the ball through to Temuri Ketsbaia. He in turn directed the ball into the path of the onrushing Hamilton who drilled the ball into the Hull net from ten yards.

Worst Moment

With Jon Dahl Tomasson equalising Paulo Di Canio's first minute opener in the Premier League fixture at Hillsborough in January 1998, it seemed all to play for going into the second half on level terms. However, in the 51st minute, a free kick was floated into the Newcastle area which Peter Atherton rose to meet, nodding it back towards the centre of the box. Des Hamilton's eyes lit up as he scuttled excitedly towards the loose ball without a plan, deciding when he got there to allow the ball to cannon off his chest and into the path of John Newsome who turned and placed the ball beyond the despairing dive of Shaka Hislop. This disappointing 2-1 defeat came less than eight months after Newcastle had finished the previous Premier League season in second. Since Kenny Dalglish's summer 'revolution', Newcastle were languishing in eleventh a full 23 points behind league leaders Manchester United.

Verdict

A Newcastle player for five years, he made almost all of his first team appearances in his first season. The last time Newcastle managed to fight off competition from Middlesbrough for a midfielder, they signed Robert Lee who went on to become a Geordie legend. This time however, although buying a promising youngster who'd racked up over eighty appearances for Bradford City, he failed to fulfil even half a per cent of that promise. Since leaving Newcastle in 2001 at the age of 25, he only managed another 52 league games whilst at Cardiff City and Grimsby Town. Along with Robert Lee, Des wasn't given a squad number by Ruud Gullit for the 1999/2000 season, though this was probably the only good decision Gullit made whilst in charge of Newcastle.

<u>1988/1989 – a year of madness</u>

Apart from the many references made in this book to the relegation season of 1988/1989, here is a small selection of those moments that made Geordies peer through a tiny gap between their fingers whilst emitting a sound not unlike that a dog makes when you stand on any part of its anatomy.

1. In the season opener against Everton at Goodison Park, new Toffees signing Pat Nevin was allowed to run with the ball unchallenged from box to box for the full ninety minutes. No tactical changes were made at any point during the game to prevent this, which culminated in a 4-0 defeat.

2. With Ian Bogie and John Hendrie tormenting the Tottenham Hotspur defence in the first home game of the season, Newcastle ended the first half two goals up. As the second half began however, it had started raining both actually and metaphorically. Straight from the kick off, Paul Walsh chipped the ball over a bemused Kevin Scott and onto the thigh of Chris Waddle. With the ball five feet from Waddle's left foot, Beasant dived to save a shot which wouldn't happen for at least another three seconds. Once the Newcastle keeper was prone, Waddle simply stretched out a leg and chipped the ball into the empty net.

3. In the second half of the same Spurs game, Mitchell Thomas managed to dispossess Darren Jackson in the centre circle. With Albert Craig in close attendance, he knocked the ball out towards Chris Waddle. Despite being within three inches of the ball throughout its journey from Thomas' foot to Waddle's, Craig decided that instead of intercepting it, he would watch to see what happened next. Craig was suddenly struck with the proverbial 'naked lunch' moment and felt a regret-fuelled burst of energy explode within him. This internal detonation of emotion caused him to chase Waddle down the wing like his entire career depended on it (it turned out that it did). Waddle took a shot at goal only to see the ball rebound off Andy Thorn. The relief on Craig's face was evident for all to see; an expression that seemed to say 'I will never *ever* let that happen to me again in my *entire* career'. However, as this thought was skating across his mind, the ball appeared at Craig's feet; "Excellent," he must have thought, "a chance to atone and prove to the crowd that I can be a super-star here." Under absolutely no

pressure whatsoever, Craig managed to misplace his pass to Ian Bogie by a distance greater than that of the distance between him and his target (scientists are still working on an equation that proves this is possible). Spurs took possession and had another shot at goal which thankfully, went wide of the post.

4.   When Newcastle played Charlton at the valley, John Cornwell managed to put in the single worst display by a Newcastle player that season. Having said that, apart from all the wild lunges, two survived penalty claims, turning his back on every free kick Charlton had around the box and all the completely mistimed challenges, he played quite well.

5.   The 2-1 win at Liverpool owed more to the ineptitude of John Aldridge to convert easy chances, the presence of a certain Michael Hooper in the Liverpool goal and the fact the referee awarded Newcastle a penalty for a challenge on Hendrie which was outside the box, than their skill with a football.

6.   John Anderson played at centre half in the home game against Charlton. As a ball was lobbed into the Newcastle penalty area, Anderson had a full five seconds to take a step back and head the ball to safety. Instead, he managed to rise a full three millimetres from the ground then turn to watch Garth Crooks outmuscle Kenny Wharton to flick the ball into the path of Robert Lee. Lee then scored the second of his three goals against Newcastle that season.

7.   The maddest of all mad moments occurred in the 2-2 home draw with Liverpool. Bruce Grobbelaar punted the ball upfield which was eventually headed on towards Newcastle's goal by Ian Rush. David McCreery gave chase and was favourite to reach the ball and clear it when he had a sudden attack of perception blindness. McCreery wasn't blessed with the longest legs in football and you'd think he'd be aware of this fact when he extended one of them towards a ball which was at least five yards ahead of him. This bizarre lack of judgment resulted in McCreery ending up in a tangle of his own limbs. The ball found John Barnes with acres of space to turn and cross into the Newcastle box. McCreery had managed to extricate himself from the previously mentioned 'web of limbs' and made his way into the box to defend the cross. The Irishman leapt at least six inches into the air and affected the flight of the ball in no way whatsoever. The ball then dropped four yards from the gaping Newcastle goal, evading a desperate lunge by John Anderson who for some reason had spread himself on the ground nowhere near the ball like a

starfish. John Aldridge arrived and swung his right foot at the ball which missed spectacularly. The ball then struck his standing leg causing him to crumple into an unchallenged heap. Shuffling on his behind, he managed to scoop the ball back towards a completely unmarked Ian Rush who then had the simplest of tasks, scooping the ball over Tommy Wright and into the top corner of the goal. Talk about bringing it on yourself.

Glyn Hodges

Toon years : 1987
Position : Midfield
Games played : 7
Goals : 0
Signed by : Willie McFaul
Transfer fee paid : £200,000

Time in Toon

Glyn's time in a black and white shirt was darker than the circles around Newcastle fans' eyes after the opening six games of the 1987/1988. With just five points on the board, Newcastle and Glyn's seventh game of the season was a 4-1 thrashing at home to Liverpool which was inevitably broadcast live to the nation on a gloomy Sunday afternoon. This game was to be Glyn's last for Newcastle which coincided with a run of just two defeats in the next eleven games without him. Hodges was a Welsh international and part of the Wimbledon side which had risen through all four divisions to become a top flight side. Newcastle manager Willie McFaul saw him as an ideal forward thinking midfielder to service the forward line of Paul Goddard and eventually, Mirandinha. Unfortunately, Glyn was mainly used as a left-sided midfielder and he pottered up and down the field with no real agenda and found himself generally ignored by his team-mates. It seemed to Newcastle fans at the time that the team would have benefitted more by placing a small traffic cone in the centre circle in lieu of the terminally bewildered Hodges.

Best Moment

Glyn did nothing of note in his seven games for Newcastle. He took a free kick in a pre-season game against Hearts from which Paul Gascoigne hit the bar and he also took the corner in the home game against Wimbledon which led to the penalty which Neil McDonald converted in a 2-1 defeat.

Worst Moment

Glyn's worst moments came in what was his final game for Newcastle versus a rampant Liverpool team boasting the recently departed Peter Beardsley, John Barnes, Barry Venison and the hat-trick scoring Steve Nicol. It was during this game that Glyn probably worked out that Willie

McFaul had signed him thinking he was somebody else. That conspiracy theory was given weight when Hodges was absent from the side for the next game and was replaced by debutant and fellow blond-haired Londoner, John Cornwell. Hodges was again asked to patrol the left side of midfield but all too often found himself covering for the perennially absent left back John Anderson who throughout the game was consistently wandering into his preferred position of centre back. Anderson, on the edge of his six yard area tried to clear a centre from John Barnes by tapping the ball directly into the path of Steve Nicol, who accepted the gift and scored.

The second goal came when Beardsley collected the ball thirty yards from goal and noticed Steve Nicol all alone out on the right wing – John Anderson again hanging around in the centre back position leaving Hodges to cover and do little to stop Nicol finding Venison who delivered the ball into the box where John Barnes headed down to the unmarked Aldridge who found the net with a volley. The third goal was a product of Peter Beardsley managing to beat the offside trap (that's assuming Newcastle were attempting to use one) and find himself alone in the box. Beardsley crossed for Nicol to slot home; a few seconds later, John Anderson appeared as if to make it clear that his was the responsibility of tracking Nicol's run. After a short interlude where Mirandinha was brought down and McDonald converted the resulting penalty, Nicol again found as much space as he needed down the Newcastle left, scampered into the area and lifted the ball over the advancing Gary Kelly to make it 4-1.

Verdict

Unfortunately, Glyn wasn't the only member of Wimbledon's Crazy Gang who disappointed and angered Newcastle fans. Dave Beasant brought his own brand of disillusionment to St. James' Park and the least said about Dennis Wise, the better. In the Wimbledon team of the mid-1980's, Glyn was part of a midfield largely bypassed by the pitch-length balls Dave Beasant would launch from just outside his own penalty area onto the head of John Fashanu. It is therefore wholly possible that Glyn was completely baffled when asked to receive passes to feet and play the ball along the ground to colleagues. If only George Reilly and Tony Cunningham were still at the club, he'd have felt right at home. Maybe Hodges left because he wasn't John Cornwell or maybe he realised he was in no way going to trouble Paul Gascoigne for a central midfield slot. Whichever, he did go on to become a Sheffield United legend, though his brand of boisterous meandering was more suited to their style of play in the early 1990's than whatever style Newcastle were trying to accomplish in 1987 (answers on a postcard).

Albert Luque

Toon years : 2005 - 2007
Position : Forward
Games played : 34
Goals : 3
Signed by : Graeme Souness
Transfer fee paid : £9.5 million
Transfer fee received : undisclosed

Time in Toon

Albert's introduction to Premier League football wasn't a bad one. His performance against Manchester United on his debut was promising, but as is always the case with Newcastle United, as soon as something good looks likely to happen, fate intervenes. Luque injured his hamstring in his next game, a 1-1 draw with Fulham and sat out the next few months. On his return to the first team, Newcastle lost 1-0 to Everton and 1-0 again to Wigan in what was the worst Newcastle performance for many years. Four defeats and three draws followed in the League, culminating in the dismissal of Graeme Souness. Glenn Roeder then took over as caretaker manager but decided against handing Luque a starting role in his teams for the remainder of that season. He brought him off the bench on five occasions however, one of which was during the game at the Stadium of Light where he scored. A rare feat befell two players that day; both Luque and Michael Chopra scored against Sunderland but still failed to find a cogent place in the Geordies' affections. Albert only managed to stay on the field for the full ninety minutes twice in his twenty-one Premier League appearances, being subbed in four of his six starts and brought on as a substitute in the other fifteen. It may seem strange to most Newcastle fans but at the time, there was a small contingent of die-hard supporters who believed Luque would 'come good', believed that 'form is temporary but class is permanent' and even uploaded *youtube* videos of his better moments in a *Deportivo de La Coruña* strip to try and convince other fans to 'give him a chance'.

Best Moment

Luque had both James Milner and the 18 year old Tim Krul to thank for ensuring his best moment in a Newcastle shirt was meaningful. It came in the 2006/2007 UEFA Cup group stage against Italian side Palermo who were at the time, top of the Italian league. Milner delivered a stunning cross from the left wing which Luque expertly nodded into the net. At the other end, Krul made a string of belief-defying saves to deny the Italians an equaliser.

Worst Moment

On his debut against Manchester United he followed a long pass into the opposing penalty area. With the neatest of touches, he flicked the dropping ball over Rio Ferdinand's head, leaving the defender completely helpless to prevent Luque, now in yards of space, from lashing the ball towards goal from less than six yards out. With only Edwin Van Der Sar to beat, Albert cocked his right foot and with all his might, sliced the ball out for a throw in.

Verdict

If you believe the rumours, Albert Luque's agent came to Newcastle with a figure in mind that he and his client would accept as a weekly wage. Allegedly, Freddie Shepherd offered Albert three times that figure to sign instead of first asking what figure they had in mind. Whether bemused by his £9.5 million price tag and inflated wages or destroyed by the hamstring injury he sustained in his second game for Newcastle, Luque never got going. When Sam Allardyce came to the club, he played Luque up front in pre-season and the Spaniard responded with a few well taken goals. However, the arrival of Mark Viduka and the presence of both Michael Owen and Obafemi Martins at the club meant giving Luque a sustained run in the first team at their expense was a gamble Allardyce was unwilling to take. Albert is just another player with an impressive pedigree who came to Newcastle and failed to provide anything other than a few fleeting glimpses of skill and a lot of disinterested milling about with no tangible purpose.

Darron McDonough

Toon years : 1992
Position : Midfield
Games played : 3
Goals : 0
Signed by : Kevin Keegan
Transfer fee paid : £90,000
Transfer fee received : Retired

Time in Toon

Perhaps an unfair inclusion, his presence in this book is relative in that Darron is one of only two Kevin Keegan singings from his first term as manager to appear in this book. He was signed, so rumours say, as a protest to the board who failed to back their new managerial appointment with funds to assist Newcastle's battle against relegation in the 1991/1992 season. This protest culminated in Keegan walking straight out of the ground after watching Newcastle win 3-1 against Swindon Town. Darron arrived presumably to add some steel to a midfield which contained Kevin Brock, Gavin Peacock, Liam O'Brien and Kevin Sheedy; all relatively shy in the tackle. After playing in the 1-1 draw with Grimsby, coming off the bench to replace Brian Kilcline in the 6-2 reverse at Wolves and start in the 3-2 defeat at home to Tranmere Rovers, Darron damaged his Achilles tendon and never played again.

Verdict

Kevin Keegan may have bought Darron because of his reputation for stomping around dangerously in midfield, hoping his mere presence would be enough to startle the opposition into giving the ball back to Newcastle without the need for a tackle. He may have thought he'd bought a player who would do the same job he eventually asked Barry Venison, Paul Bracewell and David Batty to do in the future. What he actually bought was a player who knew how to win the ball but not how to use it.

Like Stephane Guivarc'h, a player who is regarded as one of Newcastle United's worst ever signings, Darron only started two games and didn't really have a chance to show what he could do. I can't include Guivarc'h in this book as he scored one goal from two starts (and though he didn't score on his second start, Newcastle won 5-1) and was playing in a team bereft of cohesion or confidence due to a change of manager. A better way of describing Guivarc'h's signing is 'disappointing'; a world cup winner who never had the chance to show the Newcastle crowd why he was such an important part of the best international side in the world at the time. He certainly wasn't one of Newcastle's worst ever signings; let's face it, he could have cost Newcastle £17 million, picked up a reported £130,000 a week making less than two appearances a month in four years culminating in relegation after sixteen years in the Premier League. Newcastle also recouped the £3.5 million they'd paid Auxerre that summer when Guivarc'h moved to Glasgow Rangers. By comparison, Darron McDonough was playing in a team lifted by the recent arrival of a Newcastle legend as manager and a feel-good factor which saw Newcastle pick up 17 points from Keegan's first nine games in charge. From what Newcastle fans saw of Darron, he'd probably have been Keegan's first sale if not for the injury he picked up that ended his career.

Marcelino Elena

Toon years : 1999 - 2003
Position : Defender
Games played : 22
Goals : 0
Signed by : Ruud Gullit
Transfer fee paid : £5.8 million
Transfer fee received : Released

Time in Toon

There are no words in the English language which adequately sum up Marcelino's time as a Newcastle United player. It was remarkable for all the wrong reasons and completely and utterly bizarre – it fact, it was a mixture of the two, it was bizarkable. Marcelino is regarded as one of Newcastle's worst ever players not because of his performances on the pitch (as few and far between as they were) but because of the reasons he spent so much time off it. Despite a few niggling injuries, he played fifteen times in his first season which saw the dismissal of Ruud Gullit and the arrival of Sir Bobby Robson as manager. Ominously, he only managed 45 minutes of his debut in the 1-0 defeat by Aston Villa in August 1999. He then missed two games, played one, missed five, played three and then missed six. He featured in the 6-1 victory over Tottenham Hotspur in the FA Cup 3rd round replay in December 1999 and the 5-0 demolition of Southampton at St. James' a month later, looking like a solid and dependable central defender; something Newcastle were desperate for when it looked like they may have mounted a title challenge in the 2002/2003 season relying instead on Andy O'Brien, Steven Caldwell, Titus Bramble and, when it was already too late, Jonathon Woodgate. Marcelino failed to feature again for Newcastle after the 2-0 defeat to Charlton Athletic in February 2001 until he was released in 2003. Whilst he was in the treatment room for a number of months with an injured finger, most Newcastle fans would have been happy to give him one of theirs.

Best Moment

After some desperate searching it hasn't been possible to find anything positive Marcelino offered to Newcastle United. Memories of him wandering around the pitch looking for something to do and occasionally looking like he knew what he should be doing without actually doing it are far clearer than any that depict him doing anything that justified his galactic wages.

Worst Moment

Sir Bobby Robson had just presided over an 8-0 annihilation of Sheffield Wednesday in his first home game as manager in September 1999. On 25th September 1999 he then took his Newcastle side to Elland Road, a venue where the Geordies had only lost once in their previous six visits. Marcelino started in defence alongside fellow Gullit signings Alain Goma and Didier Domi. Warren Barton completed the line-up meaning Newcastle's back four that day had cost £18.5 million. Marcelino, although starting at centre back, spent most of the first ten minutes at right back leaving a huge space in front of Steve Harper for Lee Bowyer to run into and chip the ball over the goalkeeper into the top right hand corner. A few minutes later Michael Bridges picked the ball up forty yards from the Newcastle goal. Marcelino, whose starting position was the edge of his own box, ran out to try and dispossess him. With Marcelino now forty yards from goal, Bridges turned and played the ball into the gaping space behind Marcelino for Harry Kewell to take a touch and complete the one-two with Bridges who had left Marcelino in his wake. Bridges then thumped a shot towards goal which evaded the right glove of Steve Harper but fortunately hit the crossbar and bounced to safety.

A long ball from Nigel Martyn was contested by Marcelino near the centre circle; however, Lee Bowyer out-jumped him and then continued his run into the box. Marcelino then picked himself off the floor to watch as Erik Bakke floated a ball into Newcastle's box. The fact Warren Barton was covering for the absent Marcelino on the penalty spot allowed Harry Kewell to run unchallenged into the right-hand side of the penalty area and head the ball unchallenged into Newcastle's goal. A number of other attempted and failed challenges ended with Bridges coming close to increasing the lead further before Shearer nodded a goal back from a free kick. After the break, Dyer slipped a ball through the Leeds back-line to an unmarked Shearer who drilled the ball gleefully past Martyn to level the scores. 13 minutes from time, David Batty slid the ball between the statuesque Laurent Charvet and Alain Goma to Darren Huckerby. As Huckerby made his way into the box, Marcelino was again dragged out of position in an attempt to prevent the cross. All he managed to do however was leave another large area of grass behind him into which Michael Bridges received the cross and dispatched the ball beyond Harper to seal a 3-2 win.

After this defeat, Newcastle's back-line for the next six games contained a different centre back pairing perming any two from Nikos Dabizas, Aaron Hughes, Franck Dumas, Marcelino and Goma until Sir Bobby Robson decided enough was enough and brought Portuguese defender Helder in on loan for the rest of the season.

Verdict

He was a Spanish international when Newcastle signed him, but as with many other Ruud Gullit signings who looked good business, he turned out to be nothing but trouble. First there was John Karelse who conceded seven goals in his first two games (four at Southampton and three at home to Wimbledon). Then the talented but perennially injured Kieron Dyer whose petulance contributed to Sir Bobby Robson's dismissal by reportedly refusing to play out of position for the good of the team. Gullit also signed Franck Dumas whose beard ironically made him look like a musketeer (and play football like one). Silvio Maric whose 'genius' warrants a page in this book of his very own came next followed by Didier Domi, a talented footballer who possessed a colossal unprofessional streak, deciding to go AWOL at the beginning of 2001 until he was sold. Marcelino seemed to capitalise on the opulence of the Premier League which enabled clubs like Newcastle, who needed to sign the best players in order to compete with other big-spending clubs, to offer inflated transfer fees and wages. The amount of money some players earn could act as a demotivating factor, knowing that whatever the circumstance, they will pick up the same colossal wage whether they're in the treatment room or on the field.

Here is a solution; if a Premier League player is injured, they should be paid 25% of their weekly wage with the other 75% going into a 'supporters' fund'. At the end of the season, this fund would then be divided among those who bought a season ticket for that particular season including those who'd attended at least ten away games. The money allocated to that fan then discounts their tickets for next season. The club won't lose out as it is money they would have been giving to the player anyway and it would stop certain players who have just signed for the money having a sneaky few weeks off by feigning injury or sitting out the entire season doing nothing whilst on full pay. Dropping to a wage of £10,000 a week whilst they're injured isn't going to affect their lavish lifestyles (cutting their cloth accordingly) and nor should it considering they earn more in a week than the fans who are funding their lifestyle earn in a year.

Going further, the club could also introduce fines for bad performances – where it is clear that the player has just gone through the motions. The player loses their wage for that week which also goes into the supporters' fund. Not only would it help improve player-fan goodwill, but imagine how many season tickets would have been free during the time Newcastle had Marcelino, Kieron Dyer, Mark Viduka, Albert Luque and Michael Owen?

Silvio Maric

Toon years : 1998 - 2000
Position : Midfield/Forward
Games played : 31
Goals : 2
Signed by : Ruud Gullit
Transfer fee paid : £3.65 million
Transfer fee received : £2 million

Time in Toon

Silvio Maric had made his name playing for his hometown club Croatia
Zagreb and appeared in all six of their Champions' League group games
in the 1997/1998 season. Whilst wearing a Newcastle shirt however, he
barely broke into a canter. He was substituted on his debut against
Everton and his replacement, George Georgiadis, equalised David
Unsworth's opener; this set the tone for the rest of his season. However
coincidental, since appearing in the 2-0 FA Cup Semi-Final victory over
Tottenham Hotspur in April 1999, Maric's next unlucky thirteen
appearances read zero wins, five draws and eight defeats (five of which
were consecutive and spelled the end of Ruud Gullit's reign as manager).
Anonymous in every single game he played under Gullit's management,
the arrival of Sir Bobby Robson in 1999 saw him have a much more
positive effect on Newcastle's results. Scoring in his fourth and sixth
games under Robson, his appearances in the first team after the 2-1
victory over Zurich read seven victories, four draws and no defeats.
    Silvio operated best behind two strikers or as part of a three man
midfield. However, Newcastle almost always played with wingers in his
first season meaning he was often played as the second striker alongside
Temuri Ketsbaia or in a difficult two-man midfield alongside the
forward-minded Gary Speed or Rob Lee. It seemed Sir Bobby had
discovered Maric's best position when playing him as part of a three-man
midfield in a 1-0 away win at Aston Villa. Alongside Rob Lee and Gary
Speed (with Nolberto Solano and Alessandro Pistone playing as wing-
backs in a five man defence) he provided the midfield creativity that
allowed Shearer and Ketsbaia the freedom to patrol the latter third of the
field. However, this tactical foray was discarded the following season in
favour of a more familiar 4-4-2.

Best Moment

Having not scored for Newcastle at all in his previous twenty games, Maric scored twice in three games. Both goals came against FC Zurich in the UEFA Cup, one in each leg. Maric was only in the starting eleven in the first leg in Switzerland because Kevin Gallacher had been signed after the European deadline and was therefore ineligible. Early in the second half with the scores tied at 0-0, Maric intercepted a terrible pass by Zurich defender Saidou Kebe, knocked the ball forward into the box and swung his left foot, firing the ball beyond the keeper for 1-0. Newcastle won the game 2-1 and then won the home leg 3-1 with another goal by Maric. This one he nodded into an empty net after Shearer's free-kick had hit the bar.

Worst Moment

Since Newcastle's last Wembley victory brought the FA Cup to Tyneside in 1955, they had since failed against Liverpool (1974), Manchester City (1976), Manchester United (1996) and Arsenal (1998). And so, with Newcastle's first five visits to Wembley bringing five victories and with them, five trophies, they were all ready to reach equilibrium with five more visits and five straight defeats. Silvio Maric came on as a second half substitute for Solano. Sheringham hit the bar with ten minutes left and the score already 2-0 in Manchester United's favour. With the minutes counting down, Griffin hit a long ball up-field which was taken down rather messily and without occasion by Duncan Ferguson who on the third attempt, nodded the ball on to Maric. He then passed the ball through David May's legs and found himself with a clear sight of goal just behind the penalty spot. Newcastle fans everywhere expected him to side-foot the ball neatly and calmly to Peter Schmeichel's right, which he did. But instead of setting up a grandstand finish in the hope of forcing extra time, Maric toe-poked the ball wide of the post sending Geordie hands onto Geordie heads up and down the country.

Verdict

Silvio was an attacking midfielder, though he was often employed in a forward role by Newcastle. It's possible that Silvio was tempted to a club he would never have otherwise considered were it not for the glittering pile of cash on offer and failed to find any real motivation to break into a sprint during a league game. It's also possible the Newcastle coaching staff had learned nothing from the failed Newcastle career of Jon Dahl

Tomasson (an attacking midfielder played out of position) by playing Maric (an attacking midfielder) out of position.

Michael Owen

Toon years : 2005 - 2009
Position : Centre Forward
Games played : 79
Goals : 30
Signed by : Graeme Souness
Transfer fee paid : £17 million
Transfer fee received : Out of contract

Time in Toon

Have you ever bought a new car that made you really happy whenever you drove it? And did that car make you excited to drive it again tomorrow when you went to bed? Did your new car then break down inexplicably every few weeks only to give you small glimmers of hope that it might be drivable the following Saturday afternoon at 3pm before breaking down again for a month or so (all the while you're paying over the odds for tax and insurance on something you can't use)? Then, when it looked like the car was finally working, you lend it to a friend (England) and it breaks within the first 5 minutes and is out of action for an entire year and then after owning it for four years of what feels like constant heartache despite the decent power to weight (goals to games) ratio and feeling like the car really should compensate you, it leaves you without saying goodbye? You don't even get any money for it; you can't even part exchange it and then you see someone else driving it and it never breaks down and it even scores goals in the Champions League?

Best Moment

Owen's stock on Tyneside hit its peak within four months of joining the club. Scoring four goals in seven games and with Newcastle sitting 10th in the table he went on to hit a perfect hat-trick (left foot, right foot and head) away against West Ham in December 2005. It took five minutes for him to find the net; Alan Shearer played the ball ahead of Owen, inviting him to follow it into the 18 yard box. Owen knocked the ball on and with his left foot struck the ball towards goal. The goalkeeper got a hand on the ball but thankfully it had enough momentum to carry on into the net for 1-0. His second came when he met Solano's cross on the edge of the six yard box with a combination of the back of his head and shoulder which was enough to divert it beyond Roy Carroll to make it 2-1 to the visitors. His third came when the West Ham goalkeeper had made a foray into the Newcastle penalty area in the dying minutes of the game with Newcastle leading 3-2. The ball was played forward to Amdy Faye who then passed the ball to an unmarked Owen in the penalty area who had the simple task of passing the ball into an empty net with his right foot.

This performance qualifies as his best moment ahead of the goals that gave Newcastle a 2-0 win over Sunderland under the reign of Kevin Keegan in 2008 simply because not one Newcastle fan felt any animosity towards Michael Owen during the West Ham game. The away support even sang 'Michael gets the ball and scores, Halleluiah' to the tune of 'Michael row the boat ashore'. Up to and including the West Ham game, Newcastle had only lost one and drawn one of the Premier League games he'd played in but only picked up the full three points once in the other nine when he was out of the side (Newcastle only scored in two of those nine games). Two games later and Michael went in for a challenge with Spurs' Paul Robinson and Anthony Gardner just before half time and failed to re-appear after the break. The damage turned out to be a broken bone in his foot which kept him out of the next 21 games. Two operations on his foot later and he came off the bench for Michael Chopra against Birmingham in a 0-0 draw but hobbled off the field at the end feeling a 'dull ache' in the same area that had troubled him since the Spurs game. It seemed at the time that Owen had come on for half an hour to appease those who saw him as England's only hope at that year's World Cup. Instead of resting him with only two games of the season left and giving him the summer to regain his fitness, he played as if this was an 'England Reserves' outing to regain fitness before turning out for the full side. Due to injury at that World Cup, Newcastle fans didn't see him in a Newcastle shirt for a full year after that cameo against Birmingham albeit for the last three games of the season, all of which Newcastle failed to win and saw the end of Glenn Roeder's time in charge of the club.

Worst Moment

Sunday 24th May 2009; a man sent off and an own goal in the final game of the Premier league season that saw Newcastle start with a point at Old Trafford but go on to win just seven games under four different managers and finish a point from safety in 18th position. The game against Aston Villa, who themselves had won just once in fifteen games, was a wholly winnable game. However, Newcastle's players seemed to accept their fate and forget to fight once Duff had stuck out a heel and deflected Gareth Barry's hopeful punt towards goal past Steve Harper. It seemed not to matter to anyone in black and white on the field what happened next, least of all Michael Owen who'd no doubt known for months where he'd be the following season and it certainly wasn't going to be in a

Newcastle strip – so why should he care? Why should he give 100% for a club who'd paid him an absolute fortune over the previous four years, most of which when he was sitting in the treatment room doing nothing but enjoying therapeutic massages? While Jonas Gutierrez wasn't even given the last twenty minutes to at least try and have a shot at goal in the second half, Michael Owen appeared for the last 24 minutes to wander around slowly, look bored to tears and wonder what colour helicopter to buy next.

Newcastle had won at Coventry in the League Cup at the beginning of the season thanks to an extra-time goal from Owen – everything looked good as Kevin Keegan appeared on Sky Sports after the game enthusing about how James Milner was to be the corner-stone of Newcastle's immediate future. A few hours later and Milner had been sold, Xisco had been signed and the departure of Kevin Keegan for the third time was confirmed. Once relegation was definite however it did spell the end of Newcastle's expenditure on players who had done it at one stage of their career and stopped altogether when they put on the Black and White stripes. Players who commanded colossal wages because of what they'd done and not because of what they were going to do. Finally, there was a change of policy.

Verdict

Poor signings litter Newcastle United's history. Some are just poor players who are soon forgotten after a couple of mediocre appearances. Some however, are players who come in for big money, raise the fans' expectations and then fail to deliver. Michael Owen came to Newcastle as one of Europe's most prolific and gifted strikers. The promise of pairing him with Alan Shearer had drool on Geordie chins up and down the country, especially with the return of Nolberto Solano on the right wing, signed from Aston Villa on transfer deadline day in August 2005.

Seven goals in Owen's first eight games helped Newcastle to six victories, a draw and a defeat. However, an injury in his tenth appearance robbed Newcastle of his services for four months. After a glittering display and two goals in a 3-0 victory over West Bromwich Albion and then a hat-trick in a 4-2 victory at West Ham, it was a devastating blow to both Newcastle's season and Graeme Souness' hopes of holding onto his job as manager. When Kevin Keegan came back to manage the club, he suffered a run of eight Premiership games without a win until he employed Owen in a withdrawn forward role, supporting Mark Viduka and Obafemi Martins against Birmingham City on 17th March 2008. Newcastle drew that game 1-1 with Owen scoring the equaliser; the team itself that night looked coherent, vibrant and suddenly full of ideas with Owen revealing a side to his game he'd never previously shown. Newcastle then went six games unbeaten with Owen scoring five in that time, including a brace against Sunderland in a 2-0 win. After three difficult years it looked like Michael Owen would finally fulfil his promise (and justify his wages) the following season. However, the resignation of Kevin Keegan three league games into the 2008/2009 season and the installation of Joe Kinnear, Chris Hughton and then Alan Shearer as manager saw Newcastle manage only six wins in the next 34 league games culminating in their relegation from the Premier League after 16 consecutive seasons.

In the 29 games Owen played after the departure of Keegan in 2008, he found the net just eight times. When he was fit and playing in a settled team, he was excellent but he had to play under six different managers and was absent for 77 of the 148 league games Newcastle played during his time at the club. The fans wouldn't have been so angry at him had he signed for another year on a dramatically reduced wage to help Newcastle return to the Premier League at the first attempt considering this shocking statistic but in 2011 after signing a one year extension to his contract at Manchester United he used Twitter to say *"Prefer playing less often in a top team than every game in a poor team. Been there and didn't enjoy it."* Newcastle fans are still scratching their heads; every game??? Considering Graeme Souness bought Celestine Babayaro, Jean Alain Boumsong, Amdy Faye and Albert Luque, Michael Owen still managed to be the biggest waste of money in Newcastle United's history.

Frank Pingel

Toon years : 1989
Position : Forward
Games played : 14
Goals : 1
Signed by : Jim Smith
Transfer fee paid : Too much

Time in Toon

With Newcastle floundering at the bottom of Division one in 1989, Willie McFaul was eventually replaced as full-time Newcastle manager by the 'Bald Eagle', Jim Smith. His brief was simple; keep Newcastle up. He began this mammoth task with some promise, winning two and drawing one of his first three games in which United scored a spectacular seven goals. This return was remarkable only for the fact Newcastle had only managed to find the net in four of the previous fifteen games. However, those seven goals all came from midfield with Kevin Brock, Michael O'Neill, John Hendrie and even Rob McDonald scoring in what seemed to be an upturn in fortunes. All Smith had to do was replace the recently departed John Robertson with a proven, strong, athletic and prolific striker in the mould of Paul Goddard who had almost single-handedly rescued Newcastle from relegation to Division Two in the 1986/1987 season, scoring ten goals in the last fourteen games of the season. With his reputation for wheeling and dealing in the transfer market, Smith turned to the unfamiliar figure of blonde Danish battering-ram Frank Pingel.

His debut at home to Charlton was almost cut short as he left the field in the first half with blood pouring from a head-wound after an accidental clash. He went on to score one goal *for* Newcastle and one *against* (a net total of none) in his thirteen starts which culminated in relegation to Division Two.

Best Moment

Newcastle took on league champions Liverpool at home, having beaten them 2-1 at Anfield earlier in the season. With the score at 1-1, Kevin Brock took a corner which floated into the six yard box at the Leazes end. Pingel rose from a clutch of bodies and, facing the wrong way, flicked his head backwards, looping the ball into Bruce Grobbelaar's net. Pingel pranced away punching the air and screaming Scandinavian profanities. Unfortunately, his goal was cancelled out a few seconds later as John

Aldridge nodded past the hapless Tommy Wright, whose first few games between the Newcastle posts after replacing Dave Beasant were dismal. However, Pingel was made to feel at home during the game as the pitch was encircled by advertising hoardings emblazoned with the names of various Scandinavian companies.

Worst Moment

With Newcastle 1-0 up through a John Hendrie goal away to Coventry, David Smith crossed into the Newcastle box. As Steve Sedgeley leapt to try and head the ball goalwards, it skimmed his head and bounced off the unfortunate, unsuspecting and crouched Frank Pingel into the unguarded far corner. Fortunately for Pingel, Newcastle went on to win the game 2-1.

Verdict

Pingel was brought to the club to provide the goals that would keep Newcastle in the top flight but despite the highs of a creditable draw against Liverpool and the wins against Coventry, Everton and Norwich, Pingel only managed to find the net once. Frank was not short of enthusiasm and did give his all for the cause, but for all his endeavour, he only managed to stir up ghostly memories of Billy Whitehurst with his frenzied exuberance. After what fans thought would be a morale boosting 2-0 win away to title chasing Norwich City, Newcastle suffered five straight defeats and finished the season rock bottom of the table with Pingel starting and then being substituted in each of the last eight games. His partnership with the wayward and disinterested Mirandinha was never going to work given that the Brazilian seemed to lose his enthusiasm for life whenever he pulled on the black and white stripes in his last six months with the club. Pingel is just one more example of a player who proved himself elsewhere (winning eleven Danish international caps and scoring five goals) but saved his very worst performances for the Newcastle faithful.

John Robertson

Toon years : 1988
Position : Forward
Games played : 16
Goals : 0
Signed by : Willie McFaul
Transfer fee paid : £750,000

Time in Toon

John Robertson became a Heart of Midlothian legend in his first spell at Tynecastle. In seven years he'd scored 106 goals in 202 games; a record that stirred interest from south of the border. Signed by Willie McFaul at the end of April 1988, he made his Newcastle debut amid much expectation against Everton in the 1988/1989 season opener at Goodison Park along with fellow new signings Dave Beasant, Andy Thorn and John Hendrie. Everton had also strengthened, spending £925,000 on the recently relegated Chelsea's Pat Nevin, signing Newcastle's Neil McDonald for £525,000 and paying £2.2 million for West Ham's Tony Cottee. The latter took exactly thirty four seconds of his debut to set the tone for Newcastle's season; scoring the simplest of tap-ins and going on to grab a hat-trick in a 4-0 win.

Newcastle managed an unexpected 2-1 success on their next trip to Merseyside, against the previous season's champions Liverpool. Despite this blip, Newcastle only managed to pick up five points from the first seven games of the season which ended McFaul's 22 year association with the club. McFaul had put John Robertson in the starting line-up for the first five games but decided to drop him to the bench for the sixth and seventh. John took to the field for the last time under McFaul's stewardship in a 3-0 home defeat to Coventry City which left Newcastle bottom of Division One.

In a nine game run which started with the Coventry defeat, Newcastle only managed to find the net three times, all in the 3-0 home win against Middlesbrough. By the start of December, Newcastle were still bottom of the First Division and the board's desperacy to find a permanent manager to take Colin Suggett out of the firing line increased. Colin, an able coach, had presided over one win, two draws and five defeats in his capacity as caretaker. John Robertson was brought off the bench in each of Colin's first four games in charge, started the next two (defeats to QPR and Arsenal) and was dropped altogether for the next three. After the 0-0 draw away to Luton Town (the sixth consecutive game in which the team had failed to score) the Newcastle board stepped up their search for an experienced manager who enjoyed a challenge. Unable to prise Geordie Howard Kendall away from Athletic Bilbao, they turned to QPR's Jim Smith. After assessing the squad and no doubt speaking to each of the players to evaluate their happiness and willingness to help Newcastle climb away from the relegation zone, it took Jim just three days to pack John Robertson back off to Hearts.

Best Moment

John was in no way responsible for any Newcastle goals, nor for preventing any opposition attacks. Newcastle were 2-0 up in the second game of the 1988/1989 season at home to Tottenham Hotspur, looking to bounce back from the 4-0 defeat at Goodison Park the previous week. In a time when dodgy tackles were often unpunished by referees, Robertson received the ball from Kenny Wharton on the Newcastle left only to be tackled from behind by Chris Fairclough who flicked out his trailing leg and looked to have kicked Robertson in the back deliberately. An incensed Robertson had to be physically restrained by his team mates and soon calmed down. The resultant free kick was floated into the path of John Hendrie who put the ball narrowly wide of Bobby Mimms left hand post from eight yards. Had Newcastle gone 3-0 up at that point in the game, perhaps the season would have had a happier ending. Instead, Tottenham managed to draw the game 2-2.

Worst Moment

John Robertson's presence on the field in a Newcastle shirt was as inspiring as a Michael Owen press conference. He seemed unable to affect the game in either a positive or a negative way and as such, impossible to select a 'worst moment'. He was technically playing as Newcastle's number 9, given Paul Goddard's departure to Derby County in the summer of 1988 and the absence of Mirandinha from three of the first four games of the season. The only thing that the memory of John Robertson's cameo at the beginning of the 1988/1989 season does is allow Newcastle fans to fully appreciate the talents of centre forwards such as Mick Quinn and David Kelly who joined the club in later seasons.

Verdict

Newcastle lost all but two of the eight league games John started for the club and neither of those two games brought a victory. Although McFaul had presided over a relatively efficacious period for Newcastle United given the decidedly chequered history since their relegation in the 1977/1978 season, the arrival of Kevin Keegan, subsequent promotion, the Jack Charlton debacle, the flirtation with relegation in the 1986/1987 season and the creditable 8th place finish the season after, he had overseen the signing of some awful players and the departure of some world class ones. In the days before the affluence of the Premier League, you would find maybe two or three world class players at the top Division One clubs (Ian Rush, Mark Hughes and David Platt for example) but mostly, the other players in the squad were average at best. Allowing the likes of Peter Beardsley, Paul Gascoigne and Paul Goddard to leave the club to then replace them with the likes of Glyn Hodges, Mirandinha, Dave Beasant and John Robertson was baffling. These actions were echoed a decade later when Kenny Dalglish turned a title challenging team boasting the likes of Les Ferdinand and David Ginola into a relegation threatened one with Des Hamilton and the 36 year-old Ian Rush. It was the departure of Paul Gascoigne in 1988 that ripped the heart out of the side, with Newcastle looking absolutely clueless in midfield and bewildered up front with the forwards starved of any meaningful service. In truth, a 25 year old Alan Shearer would have struggled to score ten goals a season for the team in which John Robertson was asked to play. John was prolific for Hearts before coming to Newcastle (one goal every two games) and slightly less so when he went back (one goal every three games) which proves he had obvious talent, but it doesn't matter how good a finisher you are, even the best in the world can't do it on their own.

Ian Rush

Toon years : 1997 - 1998
Position : Striker
Games played : 14
Goals : 2
Signed by : Kenny Dalglish
Transfer fee paid : Free
Transfer fee received : Free

Time in Toon

Amid something of a crisis at Newcastle, with the recently formed Plc putting pressure on Dalglish to balance the books, the offer of £6m from Tottenham Hotspur for the 30 year old Les Ferdinand looked too good to refuse. However, less than 24 hours after Ferdinand had shaken hands with Tottenham Hotspur manager Gerry Francis on the deal, Alan Shearer fell down in the centre of the pitch at Goodison Park and sustained an ankle ligament problem which would keep him out for the first 6 months of the season. A man of his word, Ferdinand refused to backtrack on the verbal agreement he had with Tottenham to sign although Newcastle did their best to cancel the deal and bring him back to St. James'. With Faustino Asprilla's commitment to the club in doubt and only attacking midfielders Jon Dahl Tomasson and Temuri Ketsbaia (who were both asked to play in unfamiliar forward roles) as options up-front, Dalglish had little option but to sign the 35-years-and-10-months-old Ian Rush on a free transfer.

Rush hung around in the opposition half of the field for four full Premier League games with an expression of terminal ennui etched on his moustachioed face. One of those games was an early October visit to St. James' by Tottenham Hotspur which Newcastle won 1-0 thanks to a last minute Warren Barton goal. Tottenham sported many past and future magpies that day namely Stephen Carr, Sol Campbell, Colin Calderwood, Ruel Fox, David Ginola and Les Ferdinand. The latter emerged from the tunnel after the final whistle wearing a Newcastle shirt, stood in the centre circle and received a standing ovation from all four sides of the ground. This outpouring of goodwill was in part gratitude for the 50 goals Les had scored for Newcastle over the last 2 years, but some I'm sure was an emotional and nostalgic yearning for past pleasures having just spent the last ninety minutes watching Ketsbaia, Tomasson, John Barnes and Ian Rush scampering about randomly and trying in vain to replace Ginola, Ferdinand and even Ruel Fox in the Geordies' affections.

Newcastle managed only 35 league goals that season compared to the 73, 66, 67 and 82 they'd managed in each of the previous four. Rush did manage a League Cup goal for Newcastle against then 3rd Division Hull City, but then so did Des Hamilton.

Best Moment

Newcastle somehow managed stumble into the FA Cup final in 1998. On the way there they beat the might of Stevenage Borough, Tranmere Rovers, Barnsley and Sheffield United. Newcastle's only stern test was a tricky away tie at Goodison Park against relegation threatened and injury ravaged Everton. Shaka Hislop hardly had to dirty his gloves despite the presence of England's Nick Barmby and Scottish international Duncan Ferguson in the Everton forward line. Similarly, Newcastle hardly bothered Tomas Myhre with Tino Asprilla ineffectual in what proved to be his last appearance for the club. Asprilla was withdrawn after 53 minutes and Ian Rush, Everton's chief adversary who'd scored 25 goals in 36 games against them, took his place. It was inevitable that Rush would score and he did for the second and final time in black and white.

John Beresford played a cross-field ball which Keith Gillespie hit first time into the Everton penalty area. The ball deflected off an Everton defender and held up in a muddy puddle just beyond the far post. John Barnes then played the ball back off Richard Dunne's leg, looping the ball over Everton Goalkeeper Myhre and into the path of Rush. He slid towards the ball until both he and the ball ended up in the net.

Worst Moment

John Barnes once appeared in a television commercial for an energy drink and said '*After ninety minutes of sheer hell, you're gonna get thirsty*'. When Ian Rush played a full ninety minutes for Newcastle (seven times, losing five) it was sheer hell and the fans got thirsty (why else would they go straight to the pub after the game and drink enough to forget what had happened to them that day?). Apart from the humiliations that were the 3-1 home defeat by Wimbledon (just two years after Newcastle beat them 6-0), the 4-1 reverse at Leeds United and the bafflingly humble 1-0 defeat at PSV Eindhoven in the Champions League, Ian Rush lined up alongside John Barnes for Newcastle's Quarter-Final League Cup tie against their old club Liverpool at St. James' Park. Rush, dressed in his Newcastle strip was featured on the front of the program in an 'action' shot (rumour has it, the picture was photo-shopped) but did little that night to trouble David James' goal. Rush looked on as his protégés Robbie Fowler and Michael Owen scored a goal each in extra time to send the Magpies tumbling out of the cup (again). Newcastle's team that night was made up of eight players who'd played regularly for Kevin Keegan's title challenging side in 1995/1996. Hislop in goal, Steve Watson, John Beresford, Darren Peacock and Philippe Albert at the back with David Batty, Keith Gillespie and Rob Lee in midfield. The side included a young Aaron Hughes, starting a game for the first time and going on to represent Newcastle 277 times in total. The line-up that night was completed by Ian Rush and John Barnes but Ginola and Ferdinand they were not.

Verdict

Small coffee shops, ones which don't get many customers, will try to freshen up their displays of three day old stale cakes by placing a freshly sliced strawberry nearby. The glistening bright-coloured moist ripe fruit near the emaciated stale slices of carrot cake deludes the customer into believing that the cake is as fresh as the strawberry. It isn't clear whether when Kenny Dalglish paired Ian Rush with Jon Dahl Tomasson he was hoping for the same effect. Dalglish was under some kind of illusion that because he'd won the league with Liverpool in the 1989/1990 season with John Barnes, Ian Rush and Peter Beardsley that if he had them all in the team at Newcastle, he could do it again. He just forgot to factor 'time and tide' into his equation. For the quality of the players he'd brought in for Newcastle's 1997/1998 campaign he may as well have signed some other past Liverpool title winners and Newcastle-haunters Mike Hooper, Mark Lawrenson and Graeme Souness.

In his career, Ian Rush won five First Division titles, three FA Cups, five League Cups, one European Cup and was voted PFA players' player of the year in 1984. He was top scorer for Liverpool in nine of his fifteen seasons there. He was released by Liverpool at the end of the 1995/1996 season – his last touch in a Liverpool shirt came when the ball bounced off his arm and into the path of Eric Cantona who went on to fire the ball into the Liverpool net in the FA Cup final to hand Manchester United a 1-0 win. Howard Wilkinson then signed him for Leeds but after just three goals in thirty six league games Rush was released into society once more. He then sensibly decided that at the age of 35, enough was enough; his days of scoring goals were way behind him and so decided to give up playing football – then he signed for Newcastle.

Jon Dahl Tomasson

Toon years : 1997
Position : Attacking Midfielder
Games played : 34
Goals : 4
Signed by : Kenny Dalglish
Transfer fee paid : £2.5 million
Transfer fee received : £2.5 million

Time in Toon

Whilst the mere mention of some of the players featured in this book will invoke memories of exasperation, muted dissonance and in some cases deep-rooted grief, there are some players who can summon a cauldron of conflicting emotions; Jon Dahl Tomasson is one such player. He started out at Newcastle United in promising fashion. He scored goals for fun in the pre-season friendlies that preceded the dire 1997/1998 season. He made his debut at home against Sheffield Wednesday and found himself clean through on goal after a superb ball by Temuri Ketsbaia. Tomasson burst into the opposing penalty area before feeling the breath of a Sheffield Wednesday defender on his neck. He seemed to panic, stop and run away from the ball as if it were about to explode at any moment. Luckily, Asprilla steamed in and fired the stationary ball beyond Pressman's left hand to give Newcastle a 2-1 victory.

Newcastle's record when Tomasson started games was as average as you can imagine, winning twelve, losing eleven and drawing the other four in all competitions. Newcastle scored just seventeen league goals in the seventeen league games Tomasson started, winning just six in the process. Tomasson's first goal for the club came against Leicester City when Des Hamilton's goal bound header brushed his aura and ended up in the net to level the scores at 2-2. The Newcastle fans' hope was 'once he got his first, he'd score a hat-full'. Unfortunately, his hat was tiny and had room for just three further goals. One against Derby County in the League Cup helping Newcastle to progress to the next round and one against Crystal Palace in the infamous 'last victory in London' for just over four years. His final goal for the club came in the return fixture with Sheffield Wednesday who managed to mirror the score-line on Tyneside by winning 2-1.

Best Moment

Tomasson's best moment was so very nearly an equaliser in the away game against Barcelona in the Champions' League. Receiving a pass from John Beresford on the edge of the Barcelona box, Tomasson let fly and his deflected shot beat the goalkeeper, struck the crossbar and went out for a goal-kick. Newcastle lost the game 1-0.

His moment came however, when he scored the winner against Crystal Palace at Selhurst Park in November 1997. Ketsbaia found Tomasson in the box and he fired the ball across Kevin Miller. The goalkeeper managed to get a hand on the shot but couldn't stop it rolling into the net. Newcastle won 2-1 that day but little did the fans know they wouldn't be celebrating a victory in London until 18th December 2001 some 30 games later.

Worst Moment

Sadly, his worst moment came on his debut against Sheffield Wednesday, playing behind the increasingly disillusioned Faustino Asprilla and the erratic Temuri Ketsbaia. In the first half, he picked the ball up on the edge of the centre circle and found himself with a clear run on Kevin Pressman's goal. Outpacing the Wednesday defence and with Asprilla bursting into the box alongside him, Tomasson elected to pass the ball tamely into the hands of the prone Kevin Pressman from the edge of the area.

Verdict

Newcastle beat the likes of Ajax, Atlético Madrid and Barcelona for Tomasson's signature. That was even before Newcastle had qualified for the Champions League with a second successive 2nd place finish in the Premier League. He'd scored 28 goals in 48 games for Køge BK in Denmark and 37 goals in just 78 games for Heerenveen in Holland. He was the top scorer in Holland when he penned his five year contract with Newcastle in April 1997 but as soon as the ink was dry, so was the well he'd been drawing his goals from. He simply stopped scoring for Heerenveen altogether. He soon fell from the top of the goal-scoring charts (finishing 4th) and his lack of goals even cost his side victory in that season's Dutch Cup final, losing 4-2 to Roda JC despite his goals being the sole reason they got to that final in the first place.

Tomasson had been the top goal-scorer for Heerenveen for the two seasons before he joined Newcastle. It's a shame that Dalglish decided to jettison Newcastle's most exciting swashbuckling players in favour of Des Hamilton and Ian Rush. It's saddening to wonder just how good Newcastle could have been had Kevin Keegan had a player of Tomasson's ability at his disposal, employing him in his favoured role with Rob Lee and David Batty behind him, Les Ferdinand and Alan Shearer ahead of him. Unfortunately, whether through necessity or plain cluelessness, Dalglish played various square pegs in holes that were clearly not square, and with his cautious approach meaning a lack of goals and a lack of any semblance of excitement on the pitch, it was inevitable that Newcastle were to eventually dispense of Kenny's services in favour of someone who promised to bring back sexy football; but that's another story entirely. Tomasson was a player who ended up winning league titles with Feyenoord, AC Milan and Stuttgart, a UEFA Cup with Feyenoord (scoring the winning goal in the final) and a Champions League medal with Milan. He won 112 caps in all for Denmark and scored 52 goals.

Tomasson has gone on record to claim that when Shearer eventually returned to the team in January 1998, Dalglish relegated Tomasson to the bench and sometimes even left him out of the squad altogether. This could only have been based on his form while playing as a striker, which was not his natural position. Had Tomasson stayed until Ruud Gullit took over as manager, he may have found a niche and been the mainstay of the Newcastle front line but he decided to take a wage cut and return to Holland instead.

Could have but didn't

Carl Cort

Carl had everything a forward needed; he was tall, quick and had showed promise scoring 16 goals in 73 games for Wimbledon by the age of 23. He scored on his home debut against Derby County on an August evening in 2000 but left the field injured after 32 minutes. He returned a month later, playing three times in a week before finally pulling up in the second leg of Newcastle's League Cup tie away to Leyton Orient. Surgery followed and Cort wasn't seen again for six months. When he returned he scored four goals in six games and managed to remain fit and in the team for the remainder of Newcastle's final ten games. His record read 15 games, 7 goals.

Cort left the field on the final game of the season in May 2001 having scored in a 3-0 victory over Aston Villa but would not return to action until March 2002. A second hamstring problem combined with knee and ankle problems meant he wouldn't play a competitive game for 10 months. He came on as a substitute in the 2-0 defeat away to Arsenal and then featured in the next eight games, being substituted in all of them and scoring just once. After that he started just one more game for Newcastle, the 3-3 League Cup tie in November 2002 with Everton which Newcastle lost on penalties (again).

Hugo Viana

Fans are still waiting for Hugo Viana to realise his potential as the brightest prospect in Europe. Newcastle bought the 19 year old Viana for £8.5m in 2002, fighting off competition from a list of illustrious European suitors. In his 61 games for the club he was either taken off or brought on as a substitute 51 times meaning he only started a finished a match on ten occasions. His highs included Newcastle's second goal in the Champions' League game away at Feyenoord; a game which the Magpies won 3-2 to progress to the second group stage having lost their opening three games of the group. His lows included the 1-0 home loss to Partizan Belgrade in the last qualifying round of the 2003/2004 Champions' League and his lack of a cogent challenge on Didier Drogba in the away leg of the UEFA cup Semi-Final in Marseille. One game later he was farmed out on loan to Sporting Lisbon and then Valencia to try and learn how to run and tackle, never to be seen again on St. James' doorstep.

Wayne Routledge

Making his debut in the 2-0 win against Crystal Palace in January 2010, things looked promising as he came on as a substitute and started the move that led to Newcastle's second goal. A regular starter for the rest of the season in the Championship (some would say he'd found his level) he turned out for Newcastle seventeen times before his lack of end product and stirring of the ghost of Franz Carr meant that he was packed off back to Queens Park Rangers on loan following the defeat to Stevenage Borough and the good form of Joey Barton on Newcastle's right side of midfield. Things could have been very different for Wayne if he could have been fitted with a Sat-Nav. His spatial awareness wasn't the best and he would often find himself on the cinder-track after taking on a full-back and cocking his foot back ready to cross the ball. He has been sent out on loan no fewer than four times after failing to hold down a first team place for his parent club. When Tottenham Hotspur signed him from Crystal Palace they sent him to Portsmouth and then Fulham. After signing for Aston Villa he managed two appearances for them before going out on loan to Cardiff City.

Kieron Dyer

Toon years : 1999 - 2007
Position : Midfield
Games played : 250
Goals : 36
Signed by : Ruud Gullit
Transfer fee paid : £6 million
Transfer fee received : £6 million

Time in Toon

When Ruud Gullit paid Ipswich £6,000,000 for Kieron Dyer in 1999,
Newcastle fans were expectant. That expectant feeling never left until
the moment he signed for West Ham in 2007. Dyer qualifies as one of
Newcastle's worst players for much the same reason Michael Owen does.
Both had undeniable quality on their day and both were full England
internationals but Kieron's Newcastle career was littered with constant
bouts of injury, undisclosed illnesses and at times, an alleged
unwillingness to carry out the function for which he was paid so much
money. The word enigma doesn't quite cover what was going on when
Dyer was unavailable for selection. Whatever his ailments, the Geordies
would have been a lot more sympathetic towards him and had much
fonder memories of him had they only been told the reasons why he was
missing from the starting eleven for months at a time along with full and
frank admissions of why he was allegedly unhappy to carry out the
wishes of the manager.

If the fans' opinions of Dyer's first four years at Newcastle were
split due to his moments of undeniable brilliance almost cancelling out
the blatant shows of apathy on the field, then their collective minds were
made up on a night in Barcelona in December 2002 and the nail well and
truly hammered home following reports of his reluctance to play on the
wing in a game against Middlesbrough in late 2004. In the end, four
different managers tried and failed to prise open the box of mysteries that
was Kieron Dyer.

Best Moment

Kieron's time at Newcastle was sprinkled with great moments; his first
goal for the club against Sunderland, the cheeky back-heeled goal against
Olympiakos in the UEFA Cup (a game in which he was outstanding
playing up-front alongside Alan Shearer) or the wonderful finish after
leaving the Everton midfield for dead and jinking the ball Beardsley-like
past the last defender at Goodison Park in March 2000.

Dyer's best moment however has to be the time he broke Newcastle's Southampton jinx. Newcastle fans hated going to The Dell; even more so when a certain Matthew Le Tissier was wearing a red and white striped shirt. In the old second division, Newcastle played there eleven times and won just two. In the old first division, they played thirteen games there winning just one (that victory being all the way back in 1972). In the Premier League, Newcastle visited The Dell eight times and only came back with one solitary point in 1997. Their FA Cup record was even worse – five away games, five defeats. Things didn't look good then when Newcastle were handed a third round tie against Southampton in January 2004. The only positive thought the fans could muster was that the tie would be at staged at Southampton's new St. Mary's stadium and not The Dell. Dyer provided a master-class that night, scoring the first and then mesmerising both Michael Svensson and Claus Lundekvam before tucking the ball in the far corner to score the third and hand Newcastle a 3-0 victory. After the game Sir Bobby Robson gave the press some intricate details about the state of Dyer's bowels and an operation that was needed in relation to a constipation issue. I'm aware I'm contradicting myself here, but maybe we didn't need to know *exactly* what was keeping him out of the team; as Duran Duran once said, 'Too much information'.

Worst Moment

Two aberrations spring to Geordie minds whenever Kieron Dyer's name is mentioned and neither were filmed using a handheld camera. The first is the boxing match staged at St. James' Park on 2nd April 2005 with 'team-mate' Lee Bowyer. In this home game against Aston Villa, Steven Taylor had already been sent off for a comical hand-ball and reaction that would have been at home in the deleted scenes from the film *Platoon*. The red cards shown to Dyer and Bowyer left Newcastle with eight men and they went on to lose the game 3-0. In Dyer's defence, it was Bowyer who did the squaring up (apparently annoyed that Dyer had ignored him all game, electing to pass to anyone else) although it was Bowyer who walked away from the fracas with the ripped shirt, looking worse for the encounter and sporting a facial expression that would terrify Satan.

Dyer was essentially mild-mannered on the field for Newcastle; he'd only picked up six yellow cards in his entire Newcastle career which might say more about his timid approach to getting stuck in than his ability to keep a cool head in the heat of battle. For the record, he'd been dismissed once before, in a crazy game away to Tottenham Hotspur; another game when an outfield player, Nolberto Solano, had been dismissed for a flying save on the goal line.

The second of his transgressions happened in the most illustrious of settings; the *Camp Nou* in Barcelona. Most Geordies can only ever dream of pulling the black and white stripes on and playing for their home-town club against one of the greatest football teams on Planet Earth in their own backyard. It can't be put into words what that would mean to a true fan of the club. What it meant to Newcastle-fans-made-millionaire Kieron Dyer however was clear as he spent the time it took Barcelona to take their corners, leaning nonchalantly against the post, occupying his mind with more pressing matters which could have ranged from 'I keep thinking it's Monday' to 'Where is all that shouting coming from?'. Riquelme's corner found the head of Motta who in turn directed the ball goalwards. Had this been a dead rubber at the end of a long Sunday league campaign on a windswept Chester-le-Street field, the way Dyer attempted to stop the ball going into the net would still have invoked anger from team-mates and fans alike. A blasé flick of the leg, reminiscent of Morcambe and Wise during a rendition of 'Bring me sunshine' was all the Dyer could muster. Not only that, but even if he'd tried his very best to stop the ball going into the net, he was standing a foot *behind* the line anyway, not on it, as per his instructions. Even after the goal was given, Dyer's face failed to register an expression and gave off a powerful 'can't be bothered' vibe.

Sir Bobby Robson gave an interview a few days after the resultant 3-1 defeat and said that whilst the players watched the video of Dyer's apathetic leg-spasm, some of the players laughed. The fans who'd seen the original game postponed because of torrential rain and had to somehow find money for further accommodation, grace from their employers for staying in Spain an extra day for the rearranged fixture and a way home after the game finished certainly weren't laughing. Juxtapose this with the time Newcastle found themselves perilously close to dropping out of the then second division into the third tier of English football. They faced an away game at Derby County, another game when Newcastle ended the 90 minutes with eight players on the field. Derby had just gone two goals up and as the ball rolled into the unguarded net, Alan Thompson followed it vainly, eventually grabing onto the net at the back of the goal, facing the away fans with tears in his eyes, devastated that this defeat could mean relegation. Flash forward to Dyer's leg-twitch and make your own judgment as to why it ranks as such an awful moment.

Verdict

In the six months since Graeme Souness was installed as Newcastle manager in September 2004, Dyer was quite simply outstanding, helping Newcastle to both the FA Cup Semi-Final and UEFA Cup Quarter-Finals. After a run of four goals in nine games, playing in wins over Chelsea, Liverpool and Olympiakos, the fight with Bowyer happened. Two 1-4 reverses in the cup competitions followed. Whatever his personal differences with Bowyer, allegedly electing not to pass to him for the entire game was more a slap in the face for the fans paying his wages than for Lee Bowyer.

Since the warm glow of demolishing Olympiakos 4-0 at St. James' Park, Newcastle won just twice more in the last thirteen games of that season. When Dyer scored in the away leg of the UEFA Cup Quarter-Final against Sporting Lisbon, it left Newcastle 2-0 up on aggregate with an away goal. Dyer then missed a similar opportunity to the one he scored and then limped off in the second half with a hamstring injury. Lisbon scored three goals in the last twenty minutes of the game with Dyer off the field. It was plain to see from this statistic what Dyer brought to the team but the problem was that his game often looked good but the end product rarely matched the dazzling displays of skill and out-pacing of opponents. Because of his pace, Dyer would often find himself out on the wing, although he went on record to say that he didn't like playing there because he didn't see enough of the ball. This could have been the reason he gave a lot less than 100% in games when he was playing deep or out wide. If he wasn't asked to play where he wanted to play, he seemed to want to just go through the motions and then after the game, go out and spend what he'd 'earned' on the finer things in life to console himself.

In 2007 he became West Ham's problem, playing just 22 games in 4 years after another string of injuries which included a broken leg and numerous hamstring problems. When he signed for Queens Park Rangers in 2011, nobody was surprised when he was stretchered off after three minutes of his debut with an injured foot. More than anything though, with Dyer genuinely putting pressure on David Beckham for a starting place on the right side of the England midfield at the turn of the Millennium, all the fans can do is look back and bemoan what was a complete waste of talent.

Mike Hooper

Toon years : 1993 - 1995
Position : Goalkeeper
Games played : 30
Clean Sheets : 9
Signed by : Kevin Keegan
Transfer fee paid : £550,000
Transfer fee received : Released

Time in Toon

In his short time with Newcastle United, Mike Hooper managed to take Newcastle fans on an edifying tour of their entire emotional range; from ecstasy to despair, laughter to tears, rage to confusion and back again. Hooper had been Bruce 'spaghetti legs' Grobbelaar's understudy at Liverpool for many years and became a popular figure on the Kop by ably deputising whenever Grobbelaar (who himself was prone to erratic behaviour between the posts) was unavailable. In his younger days at Anfield, his hefty frame and huge hands were key instruments in his endeavours to guard the goal behind him. However, as time wore on and the English game became more technical, he suffered when agility and sharp reflexes were replacing 'getting in the way' and 'scaring strikers' as prerequisites for success between the posts. At times, you could almost feel the cringe of anticipation on the Newcastle fans' faces whenever the opposing team had a shot at goal, bracing themselves for the sickening thud that always followed a Mike Hooper dive.

The nimble Shay Given was a capable Goalkeeper but he would often make easy saves look spectacularly hard and was shy in coming off his line for crosses. Pavel Srnicek cut a popular figure among Newcastle supporters but his game was often riddled with rudimentary errors and the back four could be found giving nervous backward glances throughout his first few years at the club. It was for this reason that Kevin Keegan needed to bring in a 'keeper who could assertively take control of his penalty area and ensure his defence felt more assurance playing in front of a confident, intelligent and incisive custodian. Seeing the big-framed Peter Schmeichel performing heroics at Manchester United and winning points on his own at times must have inspired Keegan to want to bring in a Goalkeeper of similar stature.

Hooper started well in the Newcastle first team; a clean sheet on his debut in a 2-0 win over West Ham United and another shut-out in the 2-0 victory over Aston Villa at Villa Park. Newcastle then destroyed Notts County 7-1 in the League Cup. However, Hooper's nerves were slowly minced when Newcastle suffered three straight 2-1 defeats against

Queens Park Rangers, Southampton and Wimbledon. The game at the Dell was famous for the outrageous piece of skill by Matt Le Tissier who seemed to have run beyond a nod-back but stuck out his left foot and skilfully dragged the ball from behind him and back into his path. Reaching the ball before evading a desperate lunge by Barry Venison, he knocked it over Kevin Scott's head before side-footing it past Hooper who decided to have a lie down and watch the ball roll into the far corner rather than attempt a save.

Hooper kept his place and played in the next fourteen games, keeping six clean sheets and conceding just nine goals with Newcastle winning ten and losing just two. Despite these statistics, Hooper's form suffered as he frequently fumbled crosses and made heavy work of straightforward saves. After another 2-1 defeat by Southampton which included yet another Le Tissier effort, Hooper was blamed by fans for the 2-0 defeat in the FA Cup 3rd round replay away to Luton Town. After the 4-2 defeat away at Wimbledon which followed, Hooper lost his place in the side to Pavel Srnicek and with the Czech in goal, Newcastle went on to win ten of the next fifteen games scoring a staggering thirty five goals and conceding just twelve to finish 3rd in the Premier League in their first season back in the top division. By this point Hooper's self-belief had been well and truly pulverized, milled and powdered.

Best Moment

Newcastle played Tottenham Hotspur at home on 3rd May 1995. Newcastle raced into a two goal lead within ten minutes before Spurs scored three in the space of six minutes to make it 3-2 with just 26 minutes on the clock. Srnicek conceded a penalty and got himself sent off but on came Hooper who saved Jurgen Klinsmann's effort. Peter Beardsley got one in the second half and the game ended 3-3.

Worst Moment

In the FA Cup 3rd round replay at Kenilworth Road in February 1994, a long ball forward dropped the wrong side of the Newcastle back four. John Hartson gave chase and then looked up to see the lumbering frame of Mike Hooper bearing down on him. Hartson, unfazed, allowed the ball to bounce once before cleverly dinking it around the graceless goalkeeper, who at the time was mid-star-jump, to find himself with an empty goal to roll the ball into. After making it 1-0 to Luton, Hartson sported what looked like an embarrassed and almost apologetic expression while his team mates gleefully jumped on him in celebration. Meanwhile, Hooper trudged back towards his goal, clapped his hands and shouted something along the lines of 'come on lads, never mind'.

Verdict

If a striker makes a mistake it's embarrassing. If a midfielder makes a mistake he can at least hope his defenders will bail him out. If a defender makes a mistake, their only hope is a miraculous save by the Goalkeeper or an off-side flag. If a Goalkeeper makes a mistake, it usually results in a goal.

Goalkeeping is a profession where success depends very much on state of mind. Average keepers can be found plucking twenty-yard pile-drivers out of the top corner when they're in the mood and letting thirty-yard toe-enders squirm under their body when they're not. Take Les Sealey's performance for West Ham United in the Premier League game at St. James' Park in March 1996. Newcastle spent the entire ninety minutes camped in the West Ham half of the field, finally winning the game 3-0; it's rumoured that the person tasked with keeping count of things like corners and shots at goal had to go and get his abacus out of the car at half-time. The following day, national newspapers carried an advert titled 'spot the ball' where West Ham's half of the field was filled with crosses while Newcastle's remained empty. Sealey's performance that night was nothing short of breath-taking; it was possibly the greatest performance ever seen at St. James' Park by an opposing Goalkeeper. He was one of those 'keepers along with Mark Bosnich and David James who, when in the mood, were unbeatable but prone to basic mistakes and lapses of concentration when not.

Mike's confidence suffered after a few mistakes turned into frequent blunders but once the Newcastle crowd started to turn on him, there was no way back. After the boos started, he began trying too hard which often resulted in him misjudging crosses and attempting to make easy catches and saves look spectacular, with comical effect. However, whatever he was laughing at when a camera focussed on him sitting on the Newcastle substitutes bench directly after Newcastle conceded a goal was never revealed, but it hammered the final nail into the coffin that contained his Newcastle career. He was then sent to Sunderland on loan, presumably as a form of community service.

Something borrowed, something blue

When a professional football club finds itself in a crisis mid-season brought on by injuries or lack of form, they often turn to the loan market. This consists of a pool of players who aren't good enough for their current team or are unhappy and looking for a new club. Either way, a loan player isn't going to be in the best mood or anywhere near peak condition when they turn up at their new training ground. Newcastle have had a few players on loan over the years, some with moderate success and some with very little (the 'something blue' by the way, is the fans after watching the below play).

Andy Walker

Came from Celtic, played three games, was subbed in all of them, did very little, went back to Glasgow. Typically, he went on to score 44 goals in 67 games for Bolton which helped them gain promotion to the inaugural Premier League.

David Mitchell

Newcastle had something of a crisis up-front when Jim Smith lost Mark McGhee to injury after the 2-1 defeat to Wolverhampton Wanderers at Molineux. He turned to local lad Scott Sloan, a cumbersome chap who found it hard to get to grips with the English game having spent most of his career in Scotland with Berwick Rangers. Then came Tommy Gaynor (see below) and Paul Moran; the latter appeared in his only game, a 0-0 at home to Wolves, missed a sitter and was then substituted by the returning Mark McGhee before being immediately shipped off back to Tottenham Hotspur.

Amidst all this scrounging and disappointment was the appearance of the bearded Anglo-Celtic Australian David Mitchell on loan from Chelsea. Having previously turned out for Glasgow Rangers, Eintracht Frankfurt and Feyenoord, a goal on his debut in the 1-0 home victory over Blackburn Rovers in January 1991 had fans dreaming of a brighter immediate future. However, he got injured in the next game, a 4-2 defeat at Brighton and was never seen in black and white again.

Gavin Maguire

A central defender who was taken to court over a tackle which, it was alleged, caused the knee injury which forced Tottenham Hotspur's Danny Thomas to retire from the game at the age of only 26. Maguire left QPR and went to Portsmouth where he himself suffered a knee injury. He played on, although never fully fit, and featured in three games for Newcastle United. One of the main reasons Newcastle struggled in the 1991/1992 season under Ossie Ardiles was the lack of decent defenders, relying at different times on the talents of Darren Bradshaw, Matty Appleby, Mark Stimson and the very young Steve Watson, Alan Neilson, David Roche and Alan Thompson. Welsh international Maguire was brought in to partner Kevin Scott and help stop the slide towards division 3. He played in two wins and a draw but had to return to Portsmouth as his old injury had flared up again. He eventually moved to Millwall but never managed to fully recover from his injury and he too retired at the age of 26.

The experience of being a Newcastle defender rubbed off on him though; his final international cap came in the Wales Vs. Germany European Championship Qualifier in Nurnberg. Maguire misjudged a nodded back-pass to his Goalkeeper which Rudi Völler intercepted and scored to make it 2-0. He was replaced by Gary Speed at half-time and Wales went on to lose 4-1. Wales' goal that night was scored from the penalty spot by...

Paul Bodin

When Paul Bodin started at left back for Newcastle against Port Vale in December 1991, most fans thought Mark Stimson had finally had his hair cut. Bodin had helped Ossie Ardiles' Swindon to the play-off final where they beat Sunderland but failed to gain promotion due to allegations of illegal payments. He moved to Crystal Palace and when Ardiles became manager of Newcastle United, he brought Bodin to St. James' Park to help shore up the defence. He didn't make any impact in his six appearances. Newcastle lost three, drew two and won one conceding twelve goals. His final appearance for Newcastle came in a humiliating 4-0 defeat away to Southend United.   Whether he wasn't deemed good enough or whether Newcastle couldn't afford his transfer fee, Bodin was allowed to return to Crystal Palace. In classic style though, once he left Newcastle he re-joined Swindon and went on to score twelve goals in 1992/1993 under the stewardship of Glenn Hoddle. After gaining promotion to the Premier League with Swindon, he scored a further seven. In total for Swindon, he scored 28 goals in 146 games, a record Tony Cunningham would have been proud of, from left back.

Ignacio Maria González

Quite possibly the worst ever loan signing made by any club ever in the history of time. 'Nacho' arrived at the club along with Xisco and Fabricio Coloccini. It was reported that manager Kevin Keegan had been informed about the González deal by Dennis Wise and told to look the player up on *Youtube*. Keegan resigned stating that no manager could continue in the role if player recruitment was out of their hands. Needless to say, Newcastle's season fell apart with the hiring of Joe Kinnear and eventually Alan Shearer before facing relegation to the Championship.

'Nacho' made his debut in the aftermath of Keegan's resignation, Chris Hughton taking caretaker charge of the home game against Hull City in September 2008. Despite Hull being thrashed 5-0 by Wigan the week before, Nicky Butt gave away a penalty to give Hull a 1-0 advantage at half-time. Hull, wearing white shorts that they'd borrowed off Newcastle, scored their second goal within ten seconds of a Newcastle corner; 'Nacho' appeared from the bench as a replacement for Ameobi and then Xisco scored on his debut before Danny Guthrie was sent off. González's second game came a week later when he replaced Claudio Cacapa after 82 minutes with Newcastle already 3-1 down away to West Ham United. 'Nacho' then injured his Achilles tendon and although he remained at the club for the rest of the season he never played again and was sent back to Valencia from whence he came.

Michael Bridges

A product of Wallsend Boys Club, Bridges played for Sunderland from 1995 to 1999 experiencing one relegation and one promotion in his time there. He then joined Leeds United, helping them to third in the Premier League in 1999/2000 by scoring 19 league goals but he suffered an injury in the UEFA cup that year which led to him only representing Leeds a further ten times in four years. Cue a loan move to Newcastle United. With Newcastle 3-0 up against Leicester City at St. James' Park in February 2004, Bridges replaced Alan Shearer with 79 minutes on the clock. Precisely one minute later, Les Ferdinand pulled one back for Leicester, and the game finished 3-1. Bridges came off the bench eight times in total and even started a game, against Vålerenga in the second leg of a UEFA cup 3rd round tie. Sir Bobby Robson had been a big admirer of Bridges for many years but had failed to entice him to Newcastle until Leeds had no choice but to let him go out on loan to get in some match practice. However, despite playing in a team that contained the creative talents of Kieron Dyer, Gary Speed, Lee Bowyer and Laurent Robert, he rarely got a sniff of goal and was a ghost of the player that had promised so much.

Terry Wilson

Terry arrived at St. James' from Nottingham Forest to try and help a leaky defence which had shipped 54 goals in 29 games in the 1991/1992 season. Up until Wilson's arrival, Newcastle had conceded two or more goals in 19 of those games, recording only three clean sheets. Wilson's debut ended in a 5-2 defeat away at Oxford United and he lasted only half of his second game, the 3-0 victory over Bristol City which saw Kevin Keegan's arrival as manager. Wilson's departure back to Nottingham Forest was followed by the signing of Brian Kilcline, a proper no nonsense defender who was as instrumental as David Kelly in Newcastle's miraculous escape from relegation to English football's third tier that season.

Tommy Gaynor

Newcastle's start to the 1990/1991 season did not carry on with 'more of the same' from their 3rd place finish the season before. Missing out in the play-offs to local rivals Sunderland seemed to have a huge effect on the team, the fans and the atmosphere around the club. The front pairing of Mick Quinn and Mark McGhee wasn't firing as frequently as it had previously and good results were hard to come by. Quinn hit six in the first eleven games with McGhee only finding the net three times. They only partnered each other once in the following five league games as both suffered injuries.

In came Irishman Tommy Gaynor from Nottingham Forest to deputise for long-term injury victim Mark McGhee. He came with a pedigree; signed by Brian Clough who knew a thing or two about footballers, after he watched Gaynor score a wonder-goal for Doncaster Rovers against Brighton. Gaynor helped Forest to win the League Cup in 1989 and finish 3rd in the First Division that year. Something happened to him at Forest, losing his place in the first team and playing mainly in the reserves meant he was finally allowed to move to Newcastle on loan at the end of 1990. Whatever the issues were, Tommy seemed to bring them with him to St. James' Park. His running was muted, his love of football was under question and his desire to strain ligaments for the cause was completely absent. Newcastle won on his debut against Watford, thanks to a Mick Quinn penalty. His second game saw Leicester City gain revenge for the 5-4 reverse at St. James' Park the year before, with Newcastle on the end of the same score-line. Quinn grabbed a hat-trick but a certain David Kelly managed the same feat for Leicester. It's worth noting that Gavin Peacock made his debut for Newcastle in this game but Gaynor dawdled about the Filbert Street pitch until he was replaced by Lee Clark. He did a little better in his final two games; a win at Plymouth Argyle and a draw with Gerry Francis' Bristol Rovers in which he scored, but he was then packed off back to Forest. He wasn't selected when Forest returned to Wembley to retain the League Cup in 1990 and he soon moved on to Millwall. After Gaynor left, Newcastle had to wait a further eight league games before McGhee returned to first team action. During that time they had the aforementioned David Mitchell, Paul Moran and even Steve Watson deputising up-front, winning just two in the process. Six games later Jim Smith was gone; in came Ossie Ardiles and with him, David Kelly (Ardiles' one claim to Geordie fame).

Billy Askew

Toon years : 1990
Position : Winger
Games played : 8
Goals : 0
Signed by : Jim Smith

Time in Toon

Billy Askew's time at Hull City was so different to his time in black and white stripes, it's feasible that someone may have stolen his identity just before his transfer north. He was instrumental in Hull's promotion from Division Four in the 1982/1983 season alongside the likes of Brian Marwood, future England manager Steve McClaren and future Newcastle striker Billy Whitehurst. A further promotion followed in 1985, reaching Division Two under manager Brian Horton. Askew went on to make 136 appearances for Hull in the second tier of English football in just five seasons.

Come the end of the 1989/1990 season, Jim Smith needed a spark; something to help push Newcastle United over the line and gain promotion back to Division One at the first attempt. With the spectacular failure that was the signing of Wayne Fereday and the frequent injuries suffered by John Gallacher, Jim needed a wide-man who was dependable, quick and tricky; enter local lad William Askew. Askew had picked up an injury and missed half of the previous season for Hull and City fans will tell you he was never the same player when he returned. The Tigers' management jumped at the chance to offload him to Newcastle with a six-figure sum in their back pocket.

Billy tried very hard for Newcastle being a Newcastle fan all of his life. This was evident from the amount of chasing he did, usually after he'd failed to trap the ball and had to scurry after it. It soon became apparent that his last name might actually have been a nickname based on his passing style as most of his crosses into the box went 'askew'. He did alright in his first two games, the fans allowing him a few mistakes because he was the new boy and needed to settle in. However, in his third and fourth games, his poor form got gradually worse and it soon became clear that Newcastle were carrying a passenger. The Magpies did win three of the four games in which Askew played but his errant passing coupled with the fact his first-touch was always his last-touch resulted in him being dropped from first team action. After Askew's fourth game, a 2-1 win away at Port Vale in April 1990, he suffered the biggest ignominy it was possible for any player to ever have to face. He was replaced in the starting line-up for the game against West Bromwich Albion by Wayne Fereday. However bad Fereday had been in the 1989/1990 season, Askew's performances had made him look like Chris Waddle. Although Newcastle won that game 2-1, Jim played the next six games with only Kevin Brock as a recognised wide-man providing service for Quinn and McGhee, winning three, drawing two and losing the final game away to Middlesbrough 4-1. The Middlesbrough defeat was hard to take for a number of reasons. Not only was it their worst performance of the season, saved especially for their local rivals but it had also consigned them to an anxious two legged play-off semi-final against fierce rivals Sunderland.

Best Moment

Signing for his boyhood heroes.

Worst Moment

Finishing third in the 1983/1984 season with 80 points meant promotion back to the First Division. Finishing 3rd in the 1989/1990 season with 80 points meant a two legged play-off semi-final and then a trip to Wembley to play another one of the three teams that finished the season lower in the table. The play-off semi-final second leg in May 1990 was the day the sky fell in for Newcastle fans. It was bad enough losing and missing out on promotion, but to lose to Sunderland was unthinkable.

In the game, Askew created nothing, mistimed tackles and missed one crucial header through his lack of height in the first half which put Mark Stimson in trouble and almost led to a second goal for Sunderland in the first half. Sunderland went on to win the game, went to Wembley and lost to Swindon Town. The laughter from Newcastle fans was soon halted when Swindon were punished for financial irregularities and Sunderland were promoted in their stead. Smiles on Sunderland faces didn't last long however as they were relegated again the following season on the final day with a 3-2 defeat by Peter Reid's Manchester City despite leading 2-1 at one point. As a final irony, two of the Manchester City goals that day were scored by future Sunderland Messiah Niall Quinn.

Verdict

Newcastle fans' memories of Billy Askew are of him charging about with an expression of determination, mostly without the ball. It was perhaps this over-exuberance and desire to do well that prevented him from relaxing into games and playing his normal role of busy provider. Perhaps it was the injury he suffered that reduced his effectiveness. Whatever the reason for his transformation from useful player at Hull to useless player at Newcastle, he had the chance to redeem himself for good when he played in both legs of the play-offs in 1990. Sadly, like his fellow team-mates, he failed spectacularly to trouble the Sunderland Goalkeeper Tony Norman. Sunderland took full advantage of the cloud of disappointment that hung over St. James' at the end of season and won 2-0 on aggregate. One final twist to Askew's short Newcastle story came when his final appearance for United (less than eight months after he signed) came at his old stamping ground of Boothferry Park. Typically, Hull City ran out 2-1 winners that day but ended the season bottom of the table and were relegated.

Geremi Njitap

Toon years : 2007 - 2010
Position : Midfield
Games played : 54
Goals : 3
Signed by : Sam Allardyce
Transfer fee paid : Free
Transfer fee received : Free

Time in Toon

Suffering just one defeat in 14 games, ten of them victories, Newcastle were sitting third in the Premier League at the beginning of March 2003. On a cold night near the River Tees, Middlesbrough's Franck Queudrue lobbed a ball into the Newcastle United penalty area for Geremi to nod home. It handed Middlesbrough a 1-0 victory and their first league win at the Riverside Stadium over Newcastle. It was a game that should have been staged a few weeks earlier had it not been for a few flakes of snow falling on the steps outside the ground and then melting immediately. At least the Middlesbrough players didn't ring in sick like they did before the fixture with Blackburn Rovers in the 1996/1997 season. Newcastle went on to win just three of the next nine games and ended the season in third place after their meek title challenge fizzled out.

Geremi was at Middlesbrough on loan from Real Madrid at the time and such was his form, José Mourinho signed him for Chelsea in the summer of 2003. By 2007, Geremi had won two Champions' League medals, a Spanish League, two Premier Leagues, a League Cup, an Olympic Gold Medal and two African Cup of Nations medals with Cameroon. So, when Sam Allardyce signed him from Chelsea in a deal that didn't seem to involve a transfer fee despite Geremi having a few years left on his contract, all seemed well.

It emerged later that Mourinho had had a conversation with Sir Bobby Robson during which the state of Geremi's legs was discussed. José revealed that although Geremi was 29 going on 30, his legs were 39 going on 40. This information was supposedly passed on to someone in the Newcastle United administration but, against the warning, Geremi still ended up at St. James' Park. Allardyce then made Geremi the club captain way before his influence on the dressing room could have been gauged. It was clear from Geremi's first few games that something wasn't quite right. On one occasion, he walked onto the pitch to warm up as if he'd been sitting on his right foot for an hour and he'd got pins and needles. He continued throughout the game in this fashion, limping when walking and when he burst into a jog, it turned out that (like a pensioner running for the bus) he could walk faster than he could run. By November 2007, Allardyce had started to cotton on to what he'd bought and stripped Geremi of the captaincy, handing it to Alan Smith instead. Whilst there were flashes of the ability he'd used to amass a glittering collection of medals and honours in his career, his first touch was as cushioned as a seat in level seven and injuries plagued him like his free-kick taking yips. His form improved however along with the overall form of the team when Kevin Keegan won the first game of his second spell in charge at the ninth attempt. In the Spring of 2008 he starred in the 2-0 victory over Fulham; crossing for Viduka to open the scoring and then directing his free-kick towards Owen's head in the second half for the second. In the following game away to Tottenham Hotspur, Geremi's was the pass that allowed Nicky Butt to fire in the equaliser and send Newcastle into the changing rooms at half time level at 1-1. Geremi's free kick in the second half put Newcastle ahead, providing the impetus for a 4-1 victory. He was heavily involved in the build ups to the second and third goals in the 3-0 home win over Reading and providing a sublime cross for Michael Owen to score the first in the home game against Sunderland later in the month.

Although he stayed with Newcastle after relegation and was prepared to play in the Championship, it may have been more to do with his Premiership wages than his desire to help the club.

Best Moment

Kevin Keegan maintained his 100% winning record as manager of Newcastle United versus Sunderland when they visited St. James' Park in April 2008. Keegan had managed to find the right balance after a run of eight League games without a victory followed by three wins and a draw. Michael Owen, Mark Viduka and Obafemi Martins started as a front three with Joey Barton, Nicky Butt and Geremi across the middle. It took just four minutes for Geremi to whip in a sublime cross from right wing. Owen's run completely bamboozled Paul McShane allowing him time to firmly nod the ball past the despairing dive of £9 million goalkeeper Craig Gordon. Owen then dispatched a penalty in the dying seconds of the first half to give the Magpies their sixth victory in the last seven meetings between the sides.

Worst Moment

Newcastle were about to play their fifth league game under the new Sam Allardyce regime. The previous four had been disjointed, lacking any cohesion and had all the hallmarks of a team with a number of new faces who all spoke different languages. Although the signs of the horrors to come were already there, Newcastle had managed to win two and draw the other two of the opening fixtures. Hopes were understandably high when they faced a Derby County side who were yet to register a point and had only scored one goal all season.

If you'd closed your eyes on the night Graeme Souness managed his final Newcastle game and then opened them during the Derby County game, it would have looked like nothing had changed in the two years between. To give some perspective on how bad the Newcastle United performance was that night, consider the following: in the 2007/2008 season Derby lost 4-0 to Tottenham, 6-0 to Liverpool, 5-0 to Arsenal, 5-0 to West Ham, 4-1 to Manchester United, 6-1 to Chelsea, 6-0 to Aston Villa, 4-0 to Reading and 6-2 in the return fixture with Arsenal, registering only one victory in the entire season. The victory? At home against Sam Allardyce's Newcastle United.

The less-than-mobile Geremi was paired with the less-than-mobile Nicky Butt in the middle. Rozehnal spent a lot of time trying to come out of defence with the ball but then playing it straight into the hands of the Derby goalkeeper Stephen Bywater. Geremi chased shadows and passed side-ways to Butt who in turn chased shadows and passed side-ways to Geremi. When Allardyce finally realised Newcastle were 1-0 down (about thirty five minutes after Derby scored) he took Geremi off and replaced him with Abdoulaye Faye (a defender) to try and claw back the deficit. When that didn't work, he took right-back for the night Steven Taylor off and replaced him with Habib Beye (another right back) to try and claw back the deficit. It was as bad a performance as the 2-0 home defeat by Blackburn Rovers three months earlier that had ended Glenn Roeder's tenure and had in-turn brought about the switch to the Allardyce administration. However, only five wins from the next sixteen games under big Sam saw the end of that particular revolution.

Verdict

Some players end up having to adapt their game when age or injuries finally catch up with them. Some players switch positions because they offer more to the team somewhere else on the field. Dynamic midfielders sometimes find that they have to sit back and use their 'football brain' more when their legs can't do what their brains are telling them to. When David Beckham was younger, he tried to cover every single blade of grass to help the team win games. When he hit his early 30's however, he could be found standing still on the right-hand side of the field waiting for the ball, collecting it and then spraying fifty yard passes and pin-point crosses into the penalty area. Phil Neville at Everton was converted from full-back to holding midfielder, much like Barry Venison was by Kevin Keegan. At the age of 30, Geremi shouldn't have had to be thinking of adapting his game because of encroaching age and by 30 years old, should have had enough time to work out what his best position was. Alan Smith was used in a wide right role by Sam Allardyce in his early days at the club even though a man with a lot more footballing knowledge, Alex Ferguson, had convinced Smith to drop back from Centre Forward to Central Midfield to good effect. Sam Allardyce's decisions were so baffling at times, some fans came up with the conspiracy theory that he was a Sunderland fan trying to bring the club down from within, much like the Sunderland fans theory about Steve Bruce.

Allardyce installed a huge backroom team of health and fitness specialists when he arrived but even they couldn't find a way to loosen Geremi's ever stiffening gait. Kevin Keegan seemed to be getting the best out of Geremi until his departure for the third time in 2008. After Keegan left, Geremi started a further 12 games in the Premier League with Newcastle, winning none of them and picking up a just five points along the way. He was just one of several high earners still at the club following relegation to the Championship but because Alan Smith, Kevin Nolan, Joey Barton, Fabricio Coloccini and Jonas Gutiérrez were actually 'bringing something to the party', they were retained. Damien Duff had already left and it seemed Geremi could only be sold if Newcastle could find someone who knew of Geremi's reputation but hadn't seen him play in the last three years. Thankfully, in January 2010 he moved to Turkish side Ankaragücü.

The Management

Newcastle United has had enough failed managers in recent times to make full deck of Top Trump cards. To my knowledge, no such thing exists but if they did, what would they look like...

Gordon Lee

Management Style:	No stars
Preferred Tactic:	Efficient
Tactical Style:	Workman
Best Signing:	Alan Gowling
Worst Signing:	Graham Oates
Fun/sad fact:	Sold Malcolm MacDonald

Bill McGarry

Management Style:	Autocratic
Preferred Tactic:	Authoritarian
Tactical Style:	Puritanical
Best Signing:	Peter Withe
Worst Signing:	Dennis Martin
Fun/sad fact:	More unpopular than Dennis Wise

Jack Charlton

Management Style:	Dubious
Preferred Tactic:	Hoof it long
Tactical Style:	Kick and rush
Best Signing:	George Reilly!?
Worst Signing:	Gary Megson
Fun/sad fact:	Shouted at Beardsley for being brilliant

Willie McFaul

Management Style:	Mild Mannered
Preferred Tactic:	Misadventure
Tactical Style:	Trite
Best Signing:	Paul Goddard
Worst Signing:	Dave Beasant
Fun/sad fact:	Served as Player, Coach and Manager

Ossie Ardiles

Management Style:	Optimistic
Preferred Tactic:	Diamond formation
Tactical Style:	Carpet football
Best Signing:	David Kelly
Worst Signing:	Franz Carr
Fun/sad fact:	Given little transfer money due to power struggle

Kenny Dalglish

Management Style:	Dour
Preferred Tactic:	10-0-0
Tactical Style:	Grim
Best Signing:	Gary Speed
Worst Signing:	George Georgiadis
Fun/sad fact:	Dismantled the entertainers

Ruud Gullit

Management Style:	Narcissistic
Preferred Tactic:	1-8-1
Tactical Style:	Sexy?
Best Signing:	Kieron Dyer
Worst Signing:	Marcelino
Fun/sad fact:	Preferred Paul Robinson to Alan Shearer

Graeme Souness

Management Style:	Disciplinarian
Preferred Tactic:	Tactics?
Tactical Style:	Pick eleven fit players and cross your fingers
Best Signing:	Lee Clark
Worst Signing:	Michael Owen
Fun/sad fact:	Signed Boumsong for £8 million

Sam Allardyce

Management Style: Brash
Preferred Tactic: 4-1-2-1-1-1 (at best guess)
Tactical Style: Illogical
Best Signing: Habib Beye
Worst Signing: Take your pick
Fun/sad fact: Lasted just 24 games

Joe Kinnear

Management Style: ****ing ****
Preferred Tactic: 4-****ing-4-****ing-2
Tactical Style: **** ****ing ****
Best Signing: Kevin ****ing Nolan
Fun/sad fact: He ******* in the ****

Carl Serrant

Toon years : 1998 - 2001
Position : Left Back
Games played : 7
Goals : 0
Signed by : Kenny Dalglish
Transfer fee paid : £500,000
Transfer fee received : Retired

Time in Toon

Like Kenny Hibbit and Peter Jackson, Serrant was born in Bradford, but then so was Des Hamilton so that is certainly no guarantee of quality. If those in the know were to be believed, Carl Serrant was destined for great things in the late nineties. His name had been mentioned in some quarters as a long-term replacement for Stuart Pearce as the England left-back. Both Leeds United and Liverpool showed an interest after Serrant's eye-catching game for England B against Russia in 1998 alongside Steve Watson, Les Ferdinand, Wayne Quinn and Kieron Dyer. Serrant's performance in the 4-1 win that day was enough to convince Kenny Dalglish that Serrant had all the qualities needed to step up from Second Division football with Oldham Athletic into the Premier League. However, Kenny had already inflicted Andreas Andersson, Paul Robinson and George Georgiadis on the Geordie public so they were less than overwhelmed by Carl's signing.

After two draws in the first two games of the 1998/1999 season, Dalglish left Newcastle and Ruud Gullit was brought in to replace him. The promise of discarding the dour negative football with a style of a sexier nature was never fulfilled however, mainly because Kenny had left behind players like Andreas Andersson, Paul Robinson and George Georgiadis. In hindsight, what Newcastle United should have employed was an alchemist, not a Football Manager. Gullit was more or less expected to instantly make a proverbial silk purse with only a few porcine listening organs at his disposal.

Serrant featured in what was technically Ruud Gullit's first game in charge, the 4-1 home defeat by Liverpool. Gullit reportedly left the stands to tell the coaching staff that Serrant should be substituted in favour of Warren Barton, such was the patchiness of his defensive display. It was unclear who instructed the team to line up with three at the back, but while Laurent Charvet, Stuart Pearce and Phillipe Albert were trying to understand where they were supposed to be playing,

Michael Owen was enjoying his day out. After the nightmare that was the Everton game (see below) having made just one start and one sub appearance in the two months between, Carl didn't feature for Newcastle again for a further nine months. He started the first game of the 1999/2000 season at home to Aston Villa alongside five other defenders (Warren Barton, Didier Domi, Franck Dumas, Marcelino and Alain Goma). Alan Shearer was red carded and Newcastle lost the game 1-0. Serrant was left on the bench for the second game of the season, a 3-1 defeat away at Tottenham Hotspur but started in the third, the 4-2 defeat at Southampton which was the penultimate nail in Gullit's managerial coffin. An injury forced Serrant off the pitch after 16 minutes and he only managed one more appearance in a Newcastle shirt.

Worst Moment

Goodison Park, Monday 23rd November 1998. It was a cold, dark evening as Sky broadcast the Premier League fixture against Everton to the nation and beyond. Ruud Gullit had overseen ten league games since his appointment as Manager three months earlier. Counting the home defeat against Liverpool, he'd overseen four wins, five defeats and two draws which left Newcastle in 13th place with sixteen points. Alan Shearer was sitting in the stand injured and Everton striker Duncan Ferguson was suspended meaning neither side had much to offer up-front. Going into this fixture, Everton had only won two of their previous thirteen league games and sat fourth bottom of the table; it was clear to the perennial Geordie pessimist in all of us what was about to happen.

Newcastle fans were in for a treat that night, watching no less than three of the players featured in this book ambling around and trying to look interested in proceedings. Up front, the dynamic duo of Andreas Andersson and Paul Dalglish, Carl Serrant at left back and to plunge the travelling supporters into further depression, Garry Brady appeared off the bench as a second half substitute. The game kicked off with little to report until a long diagonal cross-field ball from David Unsworth found Gateshead-born Don Hutchison on the edge of the Newcastle penalty area. He headed the ball over Serrant (who had no idea what was going on) towards the by-line. An assured and more experienced defender would have tracked back and then tried to shepherd Hutchison towards the corner flag, but not Carl. Serrant made sure that he brought Hutchison down with a technically brilliant lunge; he did it with such conviction, it seemed he had been practicing it in training and finally took his chance to show the nation what he'd learned. One yellow card later, Michael Ball blasted the spot-kick beyond Shay Given with confidence to score Everton's second home league goal of the season. Newcastle fans knew they'd lost the game as early as the half-hour mark as they watched what was turning out to be as bad a performance as they'd ever seen from a Newcastle side. Little wonder a deal to bring Duncan Ferguson to Tyneside was being done behind the scenes as the game was in progress. Serrant made way for Philippe Albert at half-time as Gullit became the latest Newcastle manager to try 'three-at-the-back' and then realise that Newcastle have never and will never be able to master that particular tactic, regardless of personnel.

Verdict

Serrant may well have gone on to prove himself worthy of the Newcastle left-back slot given time and respite from injury, but it's been an area Newcastle have struggled to fill and some would say is cursed. Where Frank Clark, Alan Kennedy and John Beresford did well, Damien Duff (played out of position), Celestine Babayaro (was he a left back?), Sylvain Distin (played out of position), Olivier Bernard (the second time around), Wayne Quinn (no comment), Alessandro Pistone (Wayne Quinn with curly hair), Mark Stimson (Wayne Quinn with white hair), Paul Sweeney (Wayne Quinn with ginger hair) did not. Serrant's career was ended after several operations on his knee and after 18 months out, decided to call it a day. He did return to part-time football after a few years out of the game with Farsley in the Blue Square Premier League, which is a higher level than most of Newcastle's aforementioned left-backs managed when they left the club.

David Rozehnal

Toon years : 2007 - 2008
Position : Central Defender
Games played : 25
Goals : 0
Signed by : Sam Allardyce
Transfer fee paid : £2.9 million
Transfer fee received : £2.9 million

Time in Toon

In the 2006/2007 season, manager Glenn Roeder had quantity rather than quality when it came to defensive options. Craig Moore and David Edgar played bit parts, as did Paul Huntington and Oguchi Onyewu, the latter coming in on loan from January 2007. Alain Boumsong had left the club at the end of the previous season which left Roeder with a straight choice between Steven Taylor, Craig Ramage and Titus Bramble for the centre back pairing; the latter two often getting the nod. When Sam Allardyce turned up in the summer of 2007, he swept out the old and replaced them with more of the same. Olivier Bernard left the club after failing to make a single appearance in his second spell, Titus Bramble left to make his own way in the world after his contract ran out, Craig Moore and Celestine Babayaro departed by the side-door without ceremony and Paul Huntington was sold to Leeds United.

In an attempt to build football's equivalent of Hadrian's wall in front of Shay Given, Allardyce brought in Lyon captain Claudio Cacapa, promising youngster Jose Enrique, Bolton centre-back Abdoulaye Faye, Marseille captain Habib Beye as well as hot prospects Tamas Kadar and Ben Tozer. Unfortunately, only Faye and Beye emerged from the other end of a dark season with any credit. Allardyce also brought in Czech international David Rozehnal and things looked promising when he performed on his debut in the 3-1 victory at Bolton Wanderers with all the stylish gait and poise of a young Glenn Roeder. However, despite all the defensive additions that season, Newcastle went from shipping 47 goals in 2006/2007 to conceding a princely 65 goals in 2007/2008 and ended the season on the exact same number of points. In effect, it had taken one year, three different managers and a new owner to take Newcastle from where they were when Glenn Roeder left to exactly the same points and one place higher in the league; technically, that's progress.

Rozehnal played for the Czech Republic in the European Championships in 2004 and helped them to the semi-finals before losing to eventual winners Greece. He won a Belgian Cup and a Belgian League title with FC Bruges before signing for Paris Saint-Germain in June 2005, going on to claim their player of the year title in 2007. His impressive credentials and outstanding form had caused Allardyce to scout Rozehnal when he was manager at Bolton. It was no surprise when Big Sam made him his third signing at Newcastle after the recruitment of Mark Viduka and Joey Barton who on paper, provided an impressive 'spine' for his new side. At the age of 26 and signing a four year deal, hopes were high as Rozehnal's first few games for the club were assured and tidy albeit with a few jittery moments, the fans realising it would take time to adapt to the speed of the Premier League and offered him the benefit of the doubt. In his fifth appearance, the 1-0 defeat away at Derby County, he seemed so bewildered by the lack of any semblance of creativity in front of him that he stepped out of defence with the ball on numerous occasions and attempted to dictate the play, even finding himself with a sight of goal at one point and blazing over.

Looking steady in the following game, a 3-1 victory over West Ham, Newcastle and Rozehnal's form became sketchy. After a 2-0 defeat at Arsenal in the League Cup was followed by a 3-1 reverse against Manchester City, Rozehnal was left on the bench for the following two games. Allardyce decided to pair Cacapa and Faye at the back for the first time and they provided the foundations for successive victories over Everton (3-2) and Tottenham (3-1). Then followed the 1-4 home reverse against Portsmouth and Rozehnal was again thrust into the spotlight, replacing the seemingly injured and humiliated Cacapa after 18 minutes with Newcastle already 3-1 down. He started the next seven games through necessity, Faye, Cacapa, Taylor and Ramage were all missing for the non-performance that was a 3-0 home defeat by Liverpool, and he along with the rest of the team were visibly struggling for form and confidence. Newcastle conceded eleven goals in those seven games and the proverbial vultures started to circle St. James' Park awaiting the inevitable demise of Sam Allardyce.

After being subbed early in the second half in a poor display in the 2-2 home draw with Derby County (see below), Rozehnal started just three more games for Newcastle. The last of those games, the 0-3 defeat at the hands of Arsenal for the second time in a week, Kevin Keegan took him off after 57 minutes with Newcastle 1-0 down. This time it wasn't due to a poor display, he was replaced by Joey Barton in an attempt to provide more attacking options. Kevin Keegan then bafflingly allowed him to move on loan to Lazio at the end of the January transfer window despite failing to bring Jonathan Woodgate back to the club, losing out to his preferred choice of Tottenham Hotspur. He could probably sense what was coming.

Best Moment

Rozehnal was awarded the sponsors man-of-the-match award in his fourth appearance in the 1-0 home victory over Wigan Athletic. It was a game Newcastle dominated and although the back four were rarely tested, they looked composed and organised throughout.

Worst Moment

After the humiliating 1-0 loss to Derby earlier in the season, Newcastle contrived to find themselves 2-1 down in the return fixture. With 52 minutes on the clock, Kenny Miller seemed to walk through the ghost-like David Rozehnal and passed the ball into the net beyond Shay Given. Rozehnal was substituted six minutes later and after the game Allardyce was as diplomatic as he could have been by telling the press that Rozehnal wasn't taken off due to injury but for 'tactical reasons'. He went on to admit that Rozehnal was being outdone in the air by Derby forward and Newcastle fan Steve Howard, bringing on Steven Taylor to provide a more aerially adept centre-back pairing.

Verdict

Between May 2007 and August 2009 Newcastle released nine defenders. Either through injury, contract expiry or an attempt to drive the crippling wage bill down, players such as Steven Carr, Peter Ramage, Titus Bramble, Celestine Babayaro and Claudio Cacapa were discarded. These were players who were not good enough to attract bids from other clubs while still in contract nor justify a new contract from the club. Rozehnal came to the club just as this trend was developing and became one of a further five defenders who left the club between 2007 and 2009 for a fee. That's fourteen defenders who left the club in just two years not including the numerous other youth team players and trialists who didn't make it. Rozehnal came with a CV that ticked all the boxes, however, Newcastle fans had seen it all before. A player who came in, seemingly with all the right ingredients to succeed, only to fail to come to terms with the English game. Rozehnal shirked physical battles and this was never more obvious when he came up against Derby's Steve Howard. The ever changing defensive pairings due to injuries (so much for Allardyce's hi-tech health care) didn't help the cause either and by the time Abdoulaye Faye limped off early in the 3-1 defeat at Blackburn, having to partner right-back Habib Beye in the centre seemed a step too far. Rozenhal wasn't ready to be the key man in the middle, although he read the game well, the pressure seemed to get to him until it looked he was entirely out of his depth despite playing numerous important international games for the Czech Republic and winning several leagues and cups in his time with Bruge and PSG.

Keegan allowed Rozehnal to join Lazio on loan at the end of the January transfer window in 2008, using Faye and Beye's premature return from the African Cup of Nations as an explanation. It was revealed that Rozehnal had sought assurances that he would be playing regularly at centre back, fearing that he would lose his place in the Czech Republic squad for Euro 2008 as a result but Keegan couldn't make any promises due to his lack of form and the uncertainty that he would eventually adapt to the Premier League. It seemed he'd paid the price of Allardyce's propensity for playing people out of position with Rozehnal sometimes featuring at left and right back despite his natural position being in the centre of defence.

Shorts

Garry Brady

Over the years Spurs have managed to coax Chris Waddle, Paul Gascoigne, Les Ferdinand, Sébastien Bassong, Jermaine Jenas, Ruel Fox and David Ginola to White Hart Lane – in return Newcastle have signed Stephen Carr, Peter Garland, Mark Stimson, and Garry Brady. The only transfer fee Garry ever commanded was the £650,000 Newcastle paid for him. He'd made nine substitute appearances for Spurs but was unwilling to wait for his chance to become established as a first team regular.

Most Scottish footballers who grew up in the late 70's and early 80's held Kenny Dalglish in very high esteem so when Dalglish showed an interest in Brady, he jumped at the chance. However, Dalglish had gone by the time he got his chance in the first team. Ruud Gullit persevered with him in early 1999, giving him five starts and bringing him off the bench seven times. He was something of a lucky charm despite bringing nothing but energy to the cause. Newcastle only lost two of the games he featured in but the moment that betrays his place in Gullit's thoughts was the moment he was taken off the field in the 1-1 home draw with Arsenal in February 1999 and replaced by Robert Lee. Fit again Lee then played in Brady's stead for the rest of the season. This was the same Robert Lee to whom Gullit didn't give a squad number and was stripped of the club captaincy. If that's what he thought of Lee and he'd used Lee in favour of Brady, then the former Tottenham man's time at Newcastle was truly doomed.

Paul Dalglish

Dalglish was on the books of Celtic (his dad's former team) as a junior and then signed for Liverpool (his dad's former team) when he turned 19. He made no first team appearances at all for those two giants of football and so moved to Newcastle United (his dad's current team) for free in November 1997. He got his chance in the first team over a year later when he replaced Stephane Guivarc'h in the 5-1 away win over Coventry City. Dalglish made another couple of substitute appearances before being given a run in the first team at the expense of Temuri Ketsbaia. His ineffectual meanderings upfront could well have more to do with the fact he was relying on George Georgiadis and Stephen Glass to provide him with the service he needed, than his lack of ability. This can be borne out by looking at his strike partner Alan Shearer's worrying lack of goals in the period leading up to Dalglish's penultimate first team start for Newcastle. In the home game against Sheffield Wednesday in November 1998, Newcastle kicked off having only scored two goals in the previous five games (Dalglish incidentally had featured in all of them). Morale was low, confidence was lower and Newcastle fans hadn't seen a goal for their side for over five Premier League hours (Shearer failing to register a goal for the previous six games, a run which would stretch to 10 games when he finally found the net against Charlton in January 1999). With a completely ineffectual midfield it was up to Warren Barton (who was booed by the fans as the team was read out before the game) to try a speculative twenty-five yard effort that bounced up into the chest of Sheffield Wednesday goalkeeper Pavel Srnicek. The ball rebounded directly onto the foot of Dalglish who couldn't do anything else but put the ball into the net from six yards. That was his one and only goal for Newcastle in the League but sympathies which are based around the 'but he didn't have very good service' argument disappear when you consider his career when he left Newcastle.

He went to Bury on loan for twelve games (no goals), then to Norwich for five games (no goals). He then signed for Norwich permanently for £300k playing thirty eight times and scoring just twice. He then joined Wigan for a year (thirty five games, two goals) had trials with DC United in the USA, Preston, Burnley, Peterborough and Blackpool. Blackpool were managed by Steve McMahon (his Dad's old team mate) and signed for them on a permanent deal. Twenty seven games and one goal later he was off to Scunthorpe, Linfield, Livingston, Hibernian, Houston Dynamo and finally, because of consistent injuries, ended his career after six games for his last club Kilmarnock. Kenny Dalglish scored 230 goals in his twenty one year senior career; Paul managed 22 goals in eleven years.

Alessandro Pistone

Footballers need two ingredients to be successful. One is talent and the other is heart. Newcastle were signing a lot of players who had the tag 'the brightest prospect in …' at the time and Pistone came from Italy with exactly that label. Dalglish told John Beresford that Pistone would be first choice left back because of the £4.5 million he'd spent on him, regardless of form or which would die for the club and which would spend most of his time diving out of the way of tackles. Billed as the new Maldini, Pistone shirked almost every tackling opportunity presented to him in his first season at St. James' Park. The epitome of his time in a Newcastle shirt came when he was utterly bewildered by a long ball in the 23rd minute of the FA Cup final in 1998. As it floated over his head, he actually had a yard on Marc Overmars who managed to outmuscle the curly-haired left back (who was playing on the right hand side for reasons beyond those who use logic). Pistone then tumbled to the ground although no challenge had been made on him, allowing Overmars to continue and poke the ball through Shay Given's legs for 1-0.

Diego Gavilán

Another 'fine young talent' who came to Newcastle in the wake of the success of fellow South American Nolberto Solano was Diego Antonio Gavilán. The first Paraguayan to play in the Premier League, Gavilán suffered injuries in his time at Newcastle which limited his appearances. When he did appear he was mostly anonymous. The fans' first sighting of him came at the Stadium of Light in February 2000 when he came off the bench in the 88th minute in a 2-2 draw. He was given slightly longer in his next substitute appearance; seven minutes this time, in the 3-0 victory over Manchester United the following week. Sir Bobby Robson saw Gavilán for twenty two minutes in the 2-0 defeat to Leicester City later that month, a game in which no Newcastle United player gave more than 10%. With just five games left of Sir Bobby's ship-steadying first season and with Newcastle safe in mid-table, Gavilán was given a start against Leeds United who had just lost a Champions' League Semi-Final to Galatasaray and whose season was petering out to a 3rd place finish having led the Premier League at the turn of the Millennium.

Diego had a nailed-on opportunity to score on his full debut but had his shot well saved by Nigel Martyn. He was substituted after a performance that didn't showcase any of his purported silky skills or effervescent trickery. He was replaced by an even more ineffective player in the shape of Fumaca (see below). Gavilán started the following game against a Coventry City side who had singularly failed to win a game on their travels all season and their manager Gordon Strachan had masterminded a 0-5 defeat in their last away game. Although Gavilán managed to find the net in this game it was hardly John Barnes in the Maracanã. With the score at 1-0 following a fortunate penalty, Shearer provided a master-class in controlling a football before feeding Ketsbaia. The Georgian then threaded the ball to Gavilán who fell over as he chipped the ball beyond Magnus Hedman the Coventry goalkeeper.

In all, he wasn't built for the Premier League as the stiff breeze that often gusts around St. James' Park was enough to send him off-balance. He had a taste of what the Premier League was about when he encountered Manchester United's Jaap Stam; one minute, Gavilán was running towards goal and the next he was looking up at the sky, wondering where the stadium had gone. Even though he had a complete lack of impact on the Premier League, he was still selected for Paraguay's World Cup squads in 2002 and 2006.

Jose Antune Fumaca

Sunderland manager Peter Reid signed Milton Nunez, reportedly because he'd been 'talked up' by his agent as a future superstar. It took Reid precisely one Premier League game to realise that Nunez might not actually be a footballer and sent him back to Honduras with an out of court settlement from his agent. The man doing the 'talking up' in Fumaca's case was former Colchester United manager and Sir Bobby Robson's right-hand man Mick Wadsworth. Suffice to say, Wadsworth certainly wasn't Sir Bobby's equivalent of Brian Clough's assistant Peter Taylor. Wadsworth had been manager at Colchester for just under eight months during which time he managed to glean enough knowledge to recommend both Fumaca and Lomana LuaLua to Sir Bobby.

      This wasn't a case of Newcastle going to South America and bringing back a player who needed time to settle in a new country. In his fleeting performances for Newcastle he looked like a new-comer to a football summer school, learning such skills as 'trapping a ball', 'finding space' and 'passing to a team-mate' on the job. He soon gained the nickname 'Formica' from the fans which was slightly unfair on heat resistant plastic laminate with melamine resin.

Georgios Georgiadis

Georgios played for Greek giants Panathinaikos between 1993 and 1998, winning two Greek League titles, two Greek Cups and two Greek Supercups. He was even voted Greek footballer of the year in 1995. He came to Newcastle in 1998 for half a million pounds to join fellow Greek Nicos Dabizas and offer a creative outlet alongside Kenny Dalglish's other two canny signings, Dietmar Hamman and Nolberto Solano. Looking like a young Frankie Valli, Georgios took to the field for his debut against Manchester United at Old Trafford. It was a bold move by Gullit, dropping Gary Speed after two successive defeats; 2-0 away to Tottenham and 3-0 at home to West Ham. His presence in the team coincided with two draws. Georgiadis however did nothing of note apart from play balls that were either terrible or so sublime, they were far beyond the mental capacity of his fellow team-mates to understand.

      His only goal in a Newcastle shirt came courtesy of a deflection, in the 4-1 win over Everton in the FA Cup in March 1999. Ketsbaia got two that day and Alan Shearer the other on a day when a George, a Georgian and a Geordie all scored. Thirteen games were all he managed in his season with Newcastle during which he started just eight with Newcastle winning just two. He left Tyneside and went back to sunny Greece and P.A.O.K. where he won another two Greek Cups and was part of the Greece squad that won the European Championships in 2004, sitting on the bench in the final alongside Nicos Dabizas.

Kevin Dillon

Being born in Sunderland isn't the best entry on your CV if you hope to make it in Geordieland. Making his debut at the age of 29 alongside other new signings John Gallacher, Mick Quinn, Mark McGhee and Wayne Fereday in the 5-2 home victory over Leeds United, Dillon looked like a good signing. He was combative without being spectacular. Very few players made a mark in the 1989/1990 season apart from the prolific Mick Quinn, Liam O'Brien, Mark McGhee and sometimes Kevin Brock, but Newcastle did go on to finish the season in 3rd, just missing out on automatic promotion. Comparing this season to the last promotion campaign of 1983/1984 in which Newcastle finished 3rd with the likes of Kevin Keegan, Peter Beardsley, Terry McDermott and Chris Waddle – the level of ability on show was far inferior. Dillon incurred boos from the crowd in the abject 3-2 home defeat to Oxford United in December 1989. Although he always gave his all, the smallest mistake would lead to a section of the crowd getting on his back. He wasn't selected in the starting eleven for the 0-2 home loss to Sunderland in the Play-off semi-final second leg and the following season he featured in twenty two games, of which Newcastle won nine and saw the end of Jim Smith's reign. He played one game under new boss Ossie Ardiles before being replaced in the starting line-up by Bjorn Kristensen and never seen again. He left on a free transfer, joining reading in the summer of 1991.

Dillon had scored 45 goals for former club Portsmouth, some of which had come in the top flight so Newcastle fans expected him to have a decent goals to games ratio in Division Two. It never happened. He hit the woodwork on several occasions, notably against Bournemouth and Blackburn Rovers. Dillon has one good mark on his report card however; in the summer of 1989 when Mick Quinn was out of contract, it was Dillon who called him to say that Newcastle were interested. Quinn had already spoken to Watford but chose Newcastle United instead.

Paul Robinson

On his eighth appearance for Newcastle, having come off the bench in Sir Bobby Robson's first home game in charge, he was brought down in the box by Sheffield Wednesday's Steve Haslam. Thinking he was about to register his first goal for Newcastle, and with the score already 7-0 in United's favour, Robinson grabbed the ball with a childish grin on his face. However, the smile soon vanished when he looked up and saw Alan Shearer scowling down at him. Shearer then placed the ball and thumped it into the back of the net for 8-0.

Robinson was also preferred in the starting line-up to Alan Shearer in Ruud Gullit's last game in charge of Newcastle against Sunderland on a wet August evening in 1999. He did play the ball through to Dyer for the opener but did little else before being replaced on 57 minutes by Duncan Ferguson. He managed one goal, in a UEFA cup game at home to CSKA Sofia. With Newcastle leading 3-1 on aggregate, Robinson completely missed his kick but the ball struck his standing leg and went in. He made most of his appearances from the bench, usually in the last ten minutes, more to run the clock down or to end whatever horror show Silvio Maric was currently enacting at the time. With Shearer, Ferguson and Kevin Gallacher all ahead of him in the pecking order, his two starts were more to do with Gullit's vendetta with Shearer than him forcing his way into the first team through merit. Although he made no impact in a Newcastle shirt whatsoever, United still managed to get £1.5 million for a player they'd paid Darlington £250,000 for two years earlier.

Francisco Jiménez Tejada

Known as Xisco to his friends, he arrived in Newcastle just as Kevin Keegan was departing. Scoring on his home debut amid torrid scenes of demonstration by the fans over the Keegan affair, he was powerless to prevent Newcastle slumping to a 2-1 defeat against Hull City in September 2008. His signing was suspicious to say the least. Providing nothing at all when he was on the pitch and despite lengthy spells of warming up in the second halves of games he was on the bench for, he was very rarely trusted to take the field. He appeared in the FA Cup 3rd round replay at home to Hull City but apart from winning a few headers and holding the ball up a bit then blasting an effort over the bar when well placed, did as much as he normally did. After a one minute cameo appearance off the bench in the 3-2 victory at the Hawthorns in February 2009 he wasn't spotted again until August by which time Newcastle were a Championship side. He came off the bench twice before leaving for sunny Spain on loan. Back he came and did the same again, coming off the bench twice in August 2010 before being sent back to sunny Spain.

Despite having several different managers in his time at Newcastle, none of them have considered him any higher than the seventh choice striker. They keep sending him out on loan but he keeps on coming back.

The worst team of all time?

A team that would strike fear in to the hearts of every Newcastle fan –

1. Dave Beasant
2. Mark Stimson
3. Wayne Quinn
4. Darron McDonough
5. Titus Bramble
6. Jean-Alain Boumsong
7. Wayne Fereday
8. Des Hamilton
9. Frank Pingel
10. Tony Cunningham
11. Albert Luque

Actually, I'd probably pay to watch this lot play together. Probably more fun than an afternoon out at the circus.

Trips, slips and quips

If any of the players featured in this book attempted to put their foot in their mouth, they'd probably miss and get injured in the process. However, here are some quotes by and about Newcastle related people who managed to get both feet in, all the way up to the ankles.

"I always used to put my right boot on first, and then obviously my right sock."
– **Barry Venison**

"A tremendous strike which hit the defender full on the arm - and it nearly came off."
– **Kevin Keegan**

"The substitute is about to come on - he's a player who was left out of the starting line-up today."
– **Kevin Keegan**

"Ruud Gullit was able to impose his multi-lingual skills on this match."
– **John Motson**

"England have the best fans in the world and Scotland's fans are second-to-none."
– **Kevin Keegan**

"Football's like a big market place and people go to the market every day to buy their vegetables."
– **Sir Bobby Robson**

"Luis Figo is totally different to David Beckham, and vice versa."
– **Kevin Keegan**

"We haven't been scoring goals, but football's not just about scoring goals. It's about winning."
– **Alan Shearer**

"You get bunches of players like you do bananas, though that is a bad comparison."
– **Kevin Keegan**

"Not many teams will come to Arsenal and get anything, home or away."
– **Kevin Keegan**

"Michael Owen to Newcastle is the biggest transfer of the season so far - and it will be until there's a bigger one."
– **Jim White**

"I've had an interest in racing all my life, or longer really."
– **Kevin Keegan**

"That would have been a goal if it wasn't saved."
– **Kevin Keegan**

"I can learn as much from Darius Vassell as he can from me - but he can learn more"
– **Andy Cole**

"We must have had 99 per cent of the match. It was the other three per cent that cost us."
– **Ruud Gullitt**

"The tide is very much in our court now."
– **Kevin Keegan**

"Michael Owen is a good goalscorer, not a natural born one - not yet. That takes time."
– **Glenn Hoddle**

"You can't do better than go away from home and get a draw."
 – **Kevin Keegan**

"They compare Steve McManaman to Steve Heighway and he's nothing like him, but I can see why - it's because he's a bit different."
– **Kevin Keegan**

"Goalkeepers aren't born today until they're in their late twenties or thirties."
– **Kevin Keegan**

"If you don't score you are not going to win a match."
– **Sir Bobby Robson**

"We don't want our players to be monks. We want them to be better football players because a monk doesn't play football at this level."
– **Sir Bobby Robson**

"You're on your own out there with ten mates."
– **Michael Owen**

"Argentina are the second best team in the world and there is no higher praise that that."
– **Kevin Keegan**

"At this level, if five or six players don't turn up, you'll get beat."
– **Kevin Keegan**

"I can see the carrot at the end of the tunnel."
– **Stuart Pearce**

"I would not be bothered if we lost every game as long as we won the league."
– **Mark Viduka**

"In some ways, cramp is worse than having a broken leg."
– **Kevin Keegan**

"Mirandinha will have more shots this afternoon than both sides put together."
– **Malcolm Macdonald**

"Michael Owen is irreplaceable, but Sven has Emile Heskey, James Beattie, Wayne Rooney and Darius Vassell and whoever he picks can do the job."
– **David Platt**

"The first 90 minutes of the match are the most important."
– **Sir Bobby Robson**

"I don't think there's anyone bigger or smaller than Maradona."
– **Kevin Keegan**

"If Glenn Hoddle had been any other nationality, he would have had 70 or 80 caps for England."
– **John Barnes**

"If you count your chickens before they have hatched, they won't lay an egg."
– **Sir Bobby Robson**

"Nicolas Anelka left Arsenal for £23million and they built a training ground on him."
– **Kevin Keegan**

"Don't ask me what a typical Brazilian is because I don't know what a typical Brazilian is. But Romario was a typical Brazilian"
– **Sir Bobby Robson**

"We didn't underestimate them - they were just a lot better than we thought."
– **Sir Bobby Robson**

"I never make predictions and I never will."
– **Paul Gascoigne (making a prediction)**

"I'm not trying to make excuses for David Seaman but I think the lights may have been a problem."
– **Kevin Keegan (making an excuse for David Seaman)**

"Yeading was a potential banana blip for Newcastle."
– **Sir Bobby Robson**

"People will look at Bowyer and Woodgate and say ? Well, there's no mud without flames"
– **Gordon Taylor**

"Arsenal are streets ahead of everyone in this league and Manchester United are up there with them."
– **Craig Bellamy**

"The Croatians don't play well without the ball."
– **Barry Venison**

"He's very fast and if he gets a yard ahead of himself nobody will catch him."
– **Sir Bobby Robson**

"I've had 14 bookings this season, 8 of which were my fault, but 7 of which were disputable."
– **Paul Gascoigne**

"The Gillingham players have slumped to their feet."
– **Mick Quinn**

"I would not say he is the best left-winger in the Premiership, but there are none better."
– **Ron Atkinson (about David Ginola)**

"I can count on the fingers of one hand ten games where we've caused our own downfall."
– **Joe Kinnear**

"There will be a game where somebody scores more than Brazil and that might be the game that they lose."
– **Sir Bobby Robson**

"One accusation you can't throw at me is that I've always done my best."
– **Alan Shearer**

"I've never wanted to leave. I'm here for the rest of my life, and hopefully after that as well."
– **Alan Shearer**

"Leeds is a great club and it's been my home for years, even though I live in Middlesbrough."
– **Jonathan Woodgate**

"I was surprised, but I always say nothing surprises me in football."
– **Les Ferdinand**

"Ian Rush is deadly 10 times out of 10, but that wasn't one of them."
– **Peter Jones**

"I couldn't settle in Italy - it was like living in a foreign country."
– **Ian Rush**

"I don't believe in superstitions. I just do certain things because I'm scared in case something will happen if I don't do them."
– **Michael Owen**

Conclusion

Magpies are famous for collecting shiny objects, however, Newcastle United's magpies haven't collected anything shiny for over forty years now. Each Newcastle fan has his or her idea of who the worst players are, who the worst signings were and who should and shouldn't have been on the pitch. Some will stay forever loyal to the idea that Albert Luque was unlucky to suffer a hamstring tear so early in his Newcastle career from which he never recovered and refuse to include him in their worst ever eleven regardless of his performances in a black and white shirt. Some will cherish the effort put in by players like Temuri Ketsbaia and Paul Kitson while others will only remember them for never being quite as good as their peers. There are players who are universally regarded as poor but taking into consideration that Newcastle were languishing in the bottom half of the second tier of English football, the likes of Andy Hunt, Matty Appleby, Lee Makel and Franz Carr were about average for what you could expect as a fan at that time. It was when the club spent millions on players who's reputations were huge and then went on to fulfil none of their promise, or make errors you wouldn't see on a Sunday league pitch that the fans' patience was tested.

No doubt many more overpaid and overpriced footballers will darken the St. James' Park doorstep in the coming years but at least we're all safe in the knowledge that for every Lionel Pérez there'll be a Tim Krul and for every Franz Carr there'll be a David Ginola. Whoever wears the black and white shirt, we will all be divided in our opinions of who deserves to be there, who is giving his all and who should never be allowed on the pitch ever again.

Apologies to Graham Oates, Ray Blackhall and Mike Larnach who by all accounts deserve their own page in this book. However, they all played before my time so I cannot accurately depict the horror described to me by older fans in the pubs around St. James' Park. I know the book is called 'worst ever' but by comparison I cannot believe that any Newcastle player pre-1970, however bad, could be included. If you take into consideration the amount of money in the gametoday in both transfer fees and wages, and certainly since the club record transfer of Malcolm MacDonald for £185,000 in 1971, no player could be deemed a 'waste of money' before that time. Apologies also to Joey Barton, who was omitted because I want this book to be found in the 'sport' section not the 'crime' section.

If this book hasn't already made you put it down to rub your head frantically whilst rocking back and forward then let me tip you over the edge with one last name.

Archie Gourlay.

Also by Peter Nuttall

I Want To Complain : An Alternative Guide To Customer Service

Have you got something to complain about? Have you been short changed? Have you complained but got nothing but hollow apologies? Are you due compensation? Then this book could help. Instead of writing letters using red biro and block capitals, underlining every other word, swearing at inappropriate places and writing key words twice as big, follow the 'I want to complain' philosophy and make your letters entertaining; make the person dealing with your complaint want to help you instead of shoving your letter under the pile of others they have to deal with that day and getting to it 'later'.

With eight years' experience in a customer management role for a multi-national retailer, Peter realised that it was the light-hearted, entertaining letters that received the most satisfactory resolutions. 'I want to complain' explains exactly what life is like on the other end of the call-centre telephone and just how to ensure your complaints are dealt with as a priority.

The second section of the book contains a collection of genuine complaint letters Peter has written over the years using the philosophy laid out in the first section, along with their replies so you can see for yourself just how it works. Those companies written to include Marks and Spencer, Tesco, Asda and even Newcastle city council to get a parking ticket revoked - all with positive resolutions.

'I want to complain' hopes to put the 'fun' into refund and the 'jest' into goodwill gesture as it takes you on an entertaining and humorous journey into the world of customer services.

'I want to complain' was featured on Susan Calman's BBC Radio 4 feature 'The art of Complaining' in December 2011.

Playground Olympics : An alternative guide to Playground Games

Have you ever ran the 'egg and spoon race' and wondered why it's not an Olympic sport? Have you ever wondered exactly what weather the 'all-weather' pitch was designed for? Have you ever wished that the Nursery Rhyme 'Humpty Dumpty' had a happier ending? Then 'Playground Olympics : an alternative guide to playground games' has the answers.

The book explores the possible origins of the world's best known playground games such as Hot Lava (where the players will put more effort into throwing each other down the hill than they will into any other aspect of their lives) and Rounders (after the bat strikes the ball, hell literally breaks loose). There are guides to the games played in Sports Day along with sections dedicated to other aspects of school life such as a collection of 'educationally correct' nursery rhymes. If you've ever wondered what cavemen used in a game of rock, paper, scissors before paper and scissors were invented then this is the book you've been looking for.

The Wishing Tree

When Keith Knight sets out one morning to buy a loaf of bread and a tin of custard he falls into a hole outside the supermarket and ends up in a world of Dragons, Swamp Donkeys, Leprechauns and Witches. The locals soon regard him to be the 'Knight from afar' whom the prophesy foretells will lift the many curses that afflict the land. Keith, only intent on returning home must find the fabled witch, Baba Yaga, who lives in the forest of certain death. To secure a passage home, he reluctantly embarks on a quest to rid the land of the evil Mushroom King and all his heinous curses.

If you want to receive free updates on future titles by this author, send an e-mail to enquiries@peternuttall.net

Printed in Great Britain
by Amazon.co.uk, Ltd.,
Marston Gate.